Breaking the Chains of Worry and Anxiety:

Lessons from Liberty Jail with Mindfulness Therapies

Steve Davis

With Dallas Johnson, Gary Purse, and Nathan Williams

Forward by Sarah Price Hancock, MS, CRC

Illustrated by Brandon Dorman, photographs by Steve Davis

DEDICATION

Dedicated to the memory of Bryce Mack Davis

Praise for "Breaking the Chains of Worry and Anxiety"

. . . .

Steve Davis has done a wonderful service in making the powerful paradigm of Acceptance and Commitment Therapy tools accessible using a foundation of gospel principles enriched with personal insight and wisdom. – James Jackson, Registered Psychologist, Alberta, Canada

As a psychologist and member of the LDS church, I have observed a recent surge in Mormons utilizing mindfulness to manage anxiety, depression, and other mental health issues. In his book, "Breaking the Chains of Worry and Anxiety," Steve Davis effectively integrates LDS principles with empirically-supported mindfulness techniques. The dedicated reader will experience a richer understanding of the gospel while accessing cutting-edge anxiety management resources. With this unique blend, this self-help resource receives my full endorsement. – Brett T. Copeland, Psy.D., Licensed Psychologist and author of "Sexual Development & Dysfunction," University Place, Washington

"Breaking the Chains of Worry and Anxiety" could not have come at a better time for me. I was filled with fear, paralyzed even, not knowing what to do and scared I would make a wrong decision. Your book helped me break through that fear. This is such a great hands-on way to approach personal well-being because it combines wellness with faith. We are taught that faith can move mountains, so "surely our faith can cure or eliminate fear." But HOW? I have never read anything with as much practical advice about getting out of my own head that also infuses faith as a way to help and motivate. –Jocelyn Johnson, Dayton, Ohio.

"Breaking the Chains of Worry and Anxiety" is a practical resource for anyone who is looking to make progress in a Christ centered manner. Coupled with wisdom from successful people of different faiths and walks of life, the lessons learned by the prophet Joseph Smith in Liberty Jail are the vital backbone to this inspiring, effective, but most of all empowering book. – May Lundy, Salt Lake City, Utah.

"Breaking the Chains of Worry and Anxiety" will help you in your search for relief and understanding of trials both great and small. This practical book is enlightening as well as instructional in helping individuals to work though negative thought patterns and come to embrace life's anxieties with an eye towards growth and a true belief that God is over all. I feel ready to work through my difficult struggles more effectively after reading this book. – Jed Rhien, Rexburg, Idaho.

I have lived with anxiety and worry all my life and I have tried many methods, unfortunately unsuccessfully. I have never before tried methods from an LDS perspective. "Breaking the Chains of Worry and Anxiety" has been a God send. It has given me a new perspective on successfully enduring trials. I have never before reflected and pondered the time that Joseph and the brethren endured until I read the book. Reading from these pages has given me a sincere hope of freedom. Finding a "STAR" has given me the outline needed to start my road on breaking other habits which have been stumbling blocks. – Alejandra Lords, Tooele, Utah.

Having suffered from anxiety for most of my adult life I have found that anything written on the subject usually is of high interest. However, it's rare for me to find something that I can really relate to. There are so many different opinions about how to deal with anxiety, that finding the right course of action can be overwhelming. "Breaking the Chains of Worry and Anxiety" is refreshingly original because it combines faith with proven therapies. I have already experienced a positive difference in my thinking and overall mood. I only wish I had read it sooner! – Jenna Black, Rexburg, Idaho

Steve Davis's work on this sensitive subject receives my highest recommendation. This book meets a very specific need, draws on solid LDS sources as well as science-based research. I believe it will help many. – Craig Cobia, PhD, Sugar City, Idaho.

Steve Davis has done an amazing job with this book! His insights for working through problems are very helpful as he guides the reader through their own challenging trials and experiences. This amazing manual offers everything that is needed for the reader to work through emotional issues to develop a much healthier way of looking at their challenges and gain a happier state of mind. I found that I wanted to keep going and work through my challenges and felt great accomplishments as I followed his directions. This book generates a stronger desire for us to want to utilize these exercises and truly make lasting personal improvements!
– Kathy Renner, Ogden, Utah.

"Breaking the Chains of Worry and Anxiety" is a precious gift. In lieu of painstakingly searching a lifetime for answers, one can find a compilation of core objectives from mainstream experts, treatment modalities, practical application, and most importantly lessons, love, and support from the greatest teacher of them all, the Lord. The author shares a meaningful path for those looking to live a life free from the chains that bind us from reaching our true potential as children of God. – Ruby Von Dwornick, Cambridge, Massachusetts.

Contents

ACKNOWLEDGMENTS

Each of us will experience a confluence of events that will either break us, or provide the catalyst for growth—the classic refiner's fire. In this book I share very personal experiences that brought me to my knees and drove me to seek and find the gospel-centered solutions I outline in this book. I have experienced growth and healing I believe was guided by heaven and tender mercies. In many cases, the mercies were in the form of people very dear to me, who patiently helped me along my own path to healing. First is my dear wife Cynthia and my children who patiently put up with me as I worked through an extended season of affliction.

I am indebted to two counselors, Julie Shiffler and Michael Williams, who provided great advice and introduced me to solid therapies including meditation and mindfulness.

I would also like to thank my dear friends who made this book possible. First, Dr. Gary Purse who was and is my mentor on mindfulness. Second, Dr. Nathan Williams, a scholar on the prophet Joseph Smith and the author of the pattern of overcoming trials outlined in "If, Know, Therefore: Lessons from the Prophet Joseph Smith on How to Overcome All Things." Finally, Dr. Dallas Johnson who is our resident expert on Acceptance Commitment Therapy (ACT).

I owe a debt of gratitude to Arianna Mevs for her early editorial guidance and the fabulous students in Scott Cameron's senior level English Class at BYU-Idaho. These students: Lauren Baldwin, Riley Hebdon, Hannah Davis, Amelia Strommer, and Victoria McClellan, did an outstanding job. I look forward to following their careers.

I have the great blessing of being related to Brandon Dorman, a New York Times best-selling illustrator, who graciously created the book cover.

Thank you Sarah Price Hancock for your review, editorial advice, historical knowledge, passion for this topic, and the forward.

Finally, I am most grateful to my Heavenly Father and His Son Jesus Christ who provided through the Prophet Joseph Smith the pattern for healing outlined in the Lessons From Liberty Jail. I personally experienced true healing when I finally stopped grasping for quick fix remedies and followed the divine patterns set forth by His prophet.

Forward

Many members of the church wince when they hear people talk about the *Plan of Happiness,* wondering if "men are that they might have joy,"[1] do we have to wait until the next life to experience it? Mortality is specked with happiness and joy, but frequently for people living with anxiety and other symptoms not indicative of mental wellness, those specks are few and far between. Whether the person is passing through a period of situationally imposed anxiety and depression, or one more lengthy and biologically or trauma-based, it is difficult to find sensitive solution-focused, person-centered, cognitive-behavioral-therapy-type help grounded in gospel principles.

Sadly, oftentimes when members of the church finally work up the courage to seek professional help when needed, it can be difficult to find a mental health professional who has a testimony of gospel truths, resulting in receiving guidance not aligned with basic truths of the gospel. For that reason, when seeking answers to any symptoms of anxiety—in addition to getting professional help, if needed—it is crucial to remember that we have Heavenly Parents who love us, have confidence in us, and will guide us through this mortal life *if* we take time to unplug ourselves from the concept that answers are as easy and fast to find as those which instantaneously pop-up after a well-structured Internet search.

Joseph Smith discovered that answers to prayers can be delayed despite sincere desire, prayer and steady adherence to covenants. My favorite sections of the Doctrine and Covenants were received by revelation after five months of enduring frigid temperatures of a basement dungeon at Liberty Jail during what had become the most frantic time of the newly restored church's history. The prophet, Joseph, was incarcerated on false charges in an effort to appease mobs determined to "massacre every man, woman and child," if he (and other church leaders) did not go willingly.[2] During the dark winter months of 1838 and 1839, separated from his wife, children and members of the church as they were being driven from their homes by violent mobs, the prophet felt as though God's silence during this turbulent time was evidence of his distance and disregard. In

---

[1] *2 Nephi 2:25*
[2] *LeSueur, Stephen C. The 1838 Mormon War in Missouri, pg. 1.*

desperation, Joseph cried out to Heavenly Father:

> O God, where art thou? And where is the pavilion that covereth thy hiding place?

> How long shall thy hand be stayed, and thine eye, yea thy pure eye, behold from the eternal heavens the wrongs of thy people and of thy servants, and thine ear be penetrated with their cries?

> Yea, O Lord, how long shall they suffer these wrongs and unlawful oppressions, before thine heart shall be softened toward them, and thy bowels be moved with compassion toward them?[3]

In the nearly two centuries since he uttered that plea, millions of members have found peace in the Lord's response:

> My son, peace be unto thy soul; thine adversity and thine afflictions shall be but a small moment. And then, if thou endure it well, God shall exalt thee on high; thou shalt triumph over all thy foes. Thy friends do stand by thee and they shall hail thee again with warm hearts and friendly hands."[4]

Although we are not called upon to endure what Joseph did, we likely feel similar feelings of desperation when every aspect of our mortal life hits the fan in unification, feeling like they have been pushed passed their strength and distanced from those most dear. It is at these times when pain does not feel like "but a small moment," but rather a vortex of time-suspended anguish. The trick is to keep searching for answers until you find the key which unlocks that vortex so that time can continue on its natural pace. Once you find that key, share it with others.

In his book, *Breaking the Chains of Worry and Anxiety: Lessons from Liberty Jail with Mindfulness Therapies*, Steve Davis—a peer with lived experience—shares with us the key he found his personal journey to overcome anxiety and worry. He teaches us about wellness tools gathered along the way. Essentially he's providing us a very intimate look at his own search for answers to resolve anxieties and worry. Although not a mental health professional, I find his book a valuable interweaving of tools, scriptures,

---

[3] *Doctrine and Covenants 121:1-3*
[4] *Doctrine and Covenants 121:7-9*

talks, basic theoretical principles, literature, research, and personal revelation. He's polished his own struggle to help us find hope in his journey. These tools helped him understand how to create a measure of peace amidst the world's despair. It's always enlightening to learn survival skills from someone who developed the skills in life's trenches.

Steve deconstructs worries and looks at them through the gospel's lens. He takes his understanding of Acceptance and Commitment Therapy (ATC), and combines it with three principles he learned from Liberty Jail which he refers to as "If, Know and Therefore." He dissects how to:

- Accept worried thoughts and feelings
- Define personal values by which to govern a self-directed life
- Create an action plan to elevate readers as they search for their own key to release worries and anxieties.

As you take time to carefully complete the exercises in this book, I am confident that you will develop personal wellness tools which can strengthen your capacity to discover greater meaning and purpose as you tap into that confidence that comes from applying eternal principles of the gospel to obtain mental wellness. While this book is no substitute for professional care if needed, it is a perfect augmentation for anyone searching out a gospel-based perspective on loosening the chains of anxiety and worry.

—Sarah Price Hancock, MS, CRC
Psychiatric Recovery and Rehabilitation Specialist and author of the book "Recovering Hope: Essays on living successfully with mental illness"

"For all flesh is in mine hands;
be still and know that I am God"
–D&C 101:16

INTRODUCTION

BREAKING THE CHAINS OF
WORRY AND ANXIETY

I have always been drawn to the "self-help" section of any bookstore. Why? I am a classic worrier. I am not sure how it started or why, but it began when I was very young. I likely inherited it from my father and his mother. Is my worry a personality trait, a learned behavior, or something buried deep in my genetic code? The answer is a little of each. It has been a hindrance at times, and there have been seasons of affliction where my ruminations have driven me to my knees, compelling me to be humble. However, my worry has not kept me from living a happy and productive life.

A benefit of my worry is that I have spent a lot of time researching many hallmark self-improvement works, some more obscure than others. I even volunteered to teach "Principles of Personal Achievement," a college success class at Brigham Young University–Idaho, and have been teaching it for many years. In my class, I reference works like Stephen R. Covey's "The 7 Habits of Highly Effective People" or Viktor Frankl's "Man's Search for Meaning." The central text for my course is David Christensen's "Inner Victory." I have also discovered some emerging texts I believe will become future classics like Clayton Christensen's "How Will You Measure Your Life?"

Over the years of teaching personal achievement, I have come to love and believe many of the principles taught. Fortunately, for most of my life the need for real-life applications were rare. However, that dramatically changed in 2006 when I learned my younger brother had terminal brain cancer. While this news would be devastating for anyone, it hit me particularly hard. We were both infants in Southern Utah in the early 1960s. I was born in 1960, my brother in 1962. Because of our location and timing, we were both classified as "Downwinders," growing up in the path of radioactive fallout from the nuclear bomb tests conducted in Nevada. I was vaguely aware of this as a young man, but it suddenly became the proverbial elephant in the room, at least for me. I found myself not only grieving for my brother, but also trapped in worry and "what if" thinking. It didn't help to learn that my brother and his wife received a $50,000 dollar check from the federal government, basically an apology that they "didn't know" the dangers of the 1960's tests.

While the Information Age is a great blessing, it can also be a curse. I made the mistake of searching online symptoms of brain cancer and began poring through pages of digital information. I hoped that this would lead to some reassurance, but it only compounded my worry and increased my anxiety. As I was about to turn fifty, I experienced my first panic attack; I now had even more symptoms to research online. Did this lead to more peace? No! Thankfully, I turned to more traditional help and began meeting with a professional counselor. After a few weeks, my therapist suggested mindfulness and meditation, which were taught in weekly workshops held on the Brigham Young University–Idaho campus.

After my first meditation experience, I quickly went to the campus bookstore's self-help section, of course, and purchased a very large and comprehensive guide to mindfulness titled "Full Catastrophe Living" by Jon Kabat-Zin, PhD. My first book soon turned to several and I became a novice but impatient meditation student. Unfortunately, I had several internal conflicts with the mindfulness movement. First, the meditative arts and mindfulness are based on Buddhist and Hindu traditions. Also, several of the recommended books took very scientific approaches to why we struggle, usually with references to the reptile part of our brain and human tendencies of "fight or flight" passed down from our cavemen ancestors. These philosophies did not sit well with my belief that God created me.

What I discovered is a growing movement some have called "spiritual but not religious." So many are seeking peace, and they doggedly pursue it through things like meditation, mindfulness, yoga, exercise, acupuncture, nature, and so much more. In fact, it has become big business with millions subscribing to blogs, attending retreats, purchasing books, buying videos, and natural supplements. True to form, I worried I was treading down some alternative spiritual path. I yearned to be both spiritual and religious, very much in context of what President David O. McKay said when he stated, "Spirituality is the consciousness of victory over self and communion with the Infinite." Spirituality without religion is godless. My faith encouraged me to have God at the center of my healing.

MY INTRODUCTION TO "ACT"

As I pondered, prayed, and mindfully meditated, the answer from heaven was often, "Seek ye first the kingdom of God, and His righteousness; and all these things shall be added unto you."[5] I rediscovered a talk given at a Brigham Young University (BYU) Education Week by Carrie M. Wrigley, a Latter-day Saint Licensed Clinical Social Worker and counselor. The title of her talk was "Christ-Centered Healing for Depression and Low Self-Worth." Here it was, practical advice centered on the true healer, Jesus Christ. I became a huge fan of Sister Wrigley's work. On her homepage, she recommended "The Mindfulness and Acceptance Workbook for Anxiety: A Guide to Breaking Free from Anxiety, Phobias, and Worry Using Acceptance and Commitment Therapy (ACT)" by John P. Forsyth and Georg H. Eifert. I quickly ordered the book and, after reading through the text and following the prescribed homework, became a fan of ACT. On the recommendation of Dr. Dallas Johnson, an ACT specialist, I purchased a second book titled "The Happiness Trap," by Russ Harris. I found both of these resources simple to understand with practical applications.

The official practice of Acceptance and Commitment Therapy or ACT (typically pronounced as the word "act"), was founded by Steven C. Hayes and is outlined in his book "Get Out of Your Mind and Into Your Life: The New Acceptance and Commitment Therapy."[6] In "The Happiness Trap," Harris offers this definition: "It is a therapeutic intervention using acceptance and mindfulness with the goal of psychological flexibility."[7] The three core elements are:

A = Accept your thoughts

C = Choose your values

T = Take action

What I enjoyed most about the central tenet of ACT is discovering and acting on values, coupled with mindfulness and meditation practices. These

---

[5] *Matthew 6:33; 1 Nephi 13:33*
[6] *Hayes, Steven; Get Out of Your Mind and Into Your Life*
[7] *Harris, Russ. The Happiness Trap*

were very much in line with my core beliefs.

While becoming a proponent of ACT, I still yearned for a stronger spiritual connection, which I happily discovered in the spring of 2015.

IF, KNOW, THEREFORE

I had the privilege of attending a lecture by Dr. Nathan Williams titled, "If, Know, Therefore: Lessons from the Prophet Joseph Smith on How to Overcome All Things." The presentation focused on the challenges Joseph faced in Liberty Jail and the lessons he received regarding trials. As I was listening, it suddenly hit me; the prophet was being taught coping principles very much in alignment with ACT. That night, I recorded in my journal my thoughts, which served as the catalyst to create a gospel-centered self-help book to aid the growing number of Latter-day Saint members who deal with stress and anxiety.

ANXIETY ON THE RISE

Sadly, the number of people dealing with anxiety and stress continues to increase. The number of college students needing psychological help has increased in the last few years. In the 2014 National College Health Assessment, 21 percent of college students reported that they experienced anxiety to the point that it affected their academic performance, with 14 percent seeking treatment. The percentage receiving treatment for anxiety was the highest in comparison to all other mental health challenges. Citing this study, the New York Times stated:

> Anxiety has now surpassed depression as the most common mental health diagnosis among college students, though depression, too, is on the rise. More than half of students visiting campus clinics cite anxiety as a health concern . . . Nearly one in six college students has been diagnosed with or treated for anxiety within the last 12 months (emphasis added)[8].

There has also been an increase in interest on topics and practices of mental health and healing. For example, the most viewed speech on BYU's website

---

[8] *Hoffman, Jan. Anxious Students Strain College Mental Health Centers*

in 2015 was a devotional by Jonathan G. Sandberg, a marriage and family therapist and BYU professor. His talk is titled, "Healing = Courage + Action + Grace" and provides a powerful formula for dealing with anxiety.

The theories on why there is such a dramatic increase are too numerous to consider in this text. Perhaps the answer is actually found in modern scripture when the Lord revealed to Joseph Smith that in the last days "all things shall be in commotion; and surely, men's hearts shall fail them; for fear shall come upon all people."[9] Has there ever been a time of greater commotion and fear? Many struggle with worry, anxiety, and stress. Often the remedies are ineffective, temporary, or too numerous to consider.

My hope, shared by my good friends and colleagues in this project, Dr. Nathan Williams, Dr. Gary Purse, and Dr. Dallas Johnson, is that many will benefit from the lessons from pivotal moments in Church history coupled with the supporting practices of mindfulness and ACT. This book will illustrate principles with personal stories. It is our belief these lessons can inspire anyone who is dealing with worry and will provide proven strategies that will help in overcoming anxiety.

We have designed this as both a narrative and a workbook. You will get the most out of it by taking time to thoughtfully do each exercise and the associated activities. You can record your efforts in the Mindfulness Activity Log at the back of the book or download copies at http://lessonsfromlibertyjail.com.

So many of our challenges are rooted in poor habits and some of these are psychological: thinking and feeling. Og Mandino, in "The Greatest Salesman in the World," penned these words on the power of habit:

> In truth, the only difference between those who have failed and those who have succeeded lies in the difference of their habits. Good habits are the key to all success. Bad habits are the unlocked door of failure. Thus, the first law I will obey, which precedeth all others is—I will form good habits and become their slaves.[10]

These principles, if consistently applied with practice, will result in positive changes in how you think, feel, and live; as well as new habits that will help

---

[9] *Doctrine and Covenants 88:91*
[10] *Mandino, Og. The Greatest Salesman in the World*

you "break the chains of worry and anxiety."

Author's and Publisher's note

BACKGROUND

LESSONS FROM LIBERTY JAIL AND
ACCEPTANCE COMMITMENT
THERAPY (ACT)

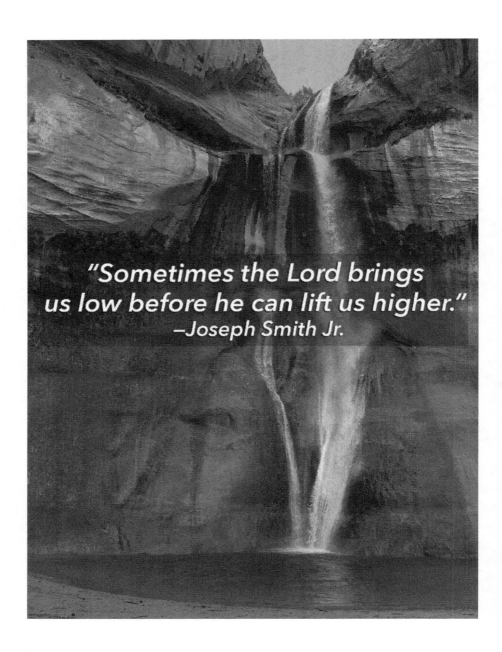

"Sometimes the Lord brings us low before he can lift us higher."
—Joseph Smith Jr.

CHAPTER 1

LESSONS FROM LIBERTY JAIL: "IF, KNOW, THEREFORE"

The Prophet Joseph Smith stated, "Deep water is what I am wont to swim in."[11] He was very familiar with tribulation. From the time of his youth in Palmyra, New York and through the entire process of translating the Book of Mormon and the restoration of the Church of Jesus Christ, he was persecuted. Later, he and his followers where driven from New York, to Ohio, then Missouri, and finally Illinois; where he was eventually martyred. While in Missouri he experienced one of his most challenging trials that lasted nearly five months in the dead of winter; his incarceration in Liberty Jail. In December of 1838, he and several other church leaders were unjustly detained and confined on trumped-up charges. Earlier in that year, the native residents of local Missouri counties became increasingly nervous as the Latter-day Saint population swelled, endangering the electoral balance. In addition, the Prophet Joseph Smith was very vocal in his opposition to slavery which rankled the pro-slavery constituents. This resulted in official petitions to the government and skirmishes between local militias and the saints which became known as the Mormon War. In response, the governor issued the Extermination Order giving official and unofficial groups license to persecute or even kill the members of the church with the end goal of driving them from the state.

Compounding their suffering, Joseph and his fellow inmates had to stand helplessly by, knowing and likely imagining the worst for their families, friends, and fellow church members. Personally, their living conditions were appalling. The rough stone prison measured only fourteen feet by fourteen feet, and the ceiling in their basement cell was only six feet tall. Since the prophet stood just over six feet, he could not stand up straight for nearly five months. He and his fellow prisoners were tormented and fed poorly. They had few visitors and limited communication with friends and family. The inmates had no bedding and slept on a stone floor with just a bit of straw. Adding to their discomfort were bitter cold

---

[11] *Doctrine and Covenants 127:2*

temperatures with estimated daily averages of 41 degrees Fahrenheit and typical lows of just over 6 degrees. In his extremity, Joseph had to have experienced the full measure of worry, anxiety, and stress. And, for several weeks, even months, Heaven was strangely absent, allowing the prophet to suffer, ponder, pray, and patiently wait. Then it came, answers from the Father through the Son, and suddenly the dungeon became what some have called the "prison temple." The personal revelations and intimate counsel were and are now canonized in sections 121–123 of the Doctrine and Covenants. In these revelations, the prophet recounts his pleadings with the Lord on behalf of the suffering saints. The answers from the Lord provides compelling and clear instructions on how to endure trials, describing the qualities of effective leaders with clear assurances that Joseph and the saints would "see the salvation of God."[12]

As mentioned in the introduction, Dr. Nathan Williams gave an inspiring presentation on the lessons learned at Liberty Jail titled "If, Know, Therefore." In his talk, he shared a pattern of overcoming found in the writings and life of the Prophet Joseph Smith.

The simple diagram that follows illustrates "If, Know, and Therefore."

If refers to unexpected trials, afflictions, and challenges inherent in mortality and our fallen state. Next comes **know**, which refers to a belief and faith in God's plan for us, including a knowledge of our divine origin and that we are children of heavenly parents. The third step is **therefore**, which refers to patterns of behavior and intentional actions inspired by this knowledge. Actions based on values will result in personal achievement and success. The culmination of this process and its ultimate blessing will be that "all these things shall give thee experience and be for thy good."[13] Throughout this text, we will build upon this model step-by-step as we incorporate the lessons from Liberty Jail and ACT.

---

[12] *Doctrine and Covenants 123:17*
[13] *Doctrine and Covenants 122:7*

In Doctrine and Covenants Section 122, the Lord gives Joseph Smith several **ifs** starting with "**if** thou art called to pass through tribulation."[14] Several of the **ifs** had to be especially poignant, since the prophet had already endured them, like being "accused of false brethren," having his "enemies fall upon [him]," and "with a drawn sword . . . tear [him] from the bosom of [his] wife, and offspring, and elder son."[15] Verse seven included possibilities of future perils, hardships, and symbolic dangers only the adversary could conjure up.

Yet in spite of all of these personally experienced and forecasted **ifs**, the prophet was reminded to "**know** thou, my son, that all these things shall give thee experience, and shall be for thy good"[16] and "God will be with you forever and ever."[17] Finally, Joseph is admonished to "**therefore**, hold on thy way . . . and fear not what man can do."[18] The final **therefore** is given when the Lord states:

> Therefore, dearly beloved brethren, let us cheerfully do all things that lie in our power; and then may we stand still, with the utmost assurance, to see the salvation of God, and for His arm to be revealed.[19]

A review of the admonitions in these two sections instructed the prophet and his followers to hold on, fear not, be cheerful, take action, be still, and, with faith, wait to see the Lord's plan.

Each of us will face our own challenges and very hard times. In fact, **if** will certainly become when. Following the prophet's example in Liberty Jail and this pattern taught by Brother Williams, we have a very simple and effective blueprint on how to overcome our challenges, including worry, anxiety, and stress.

For example, if and when I have a real personal trial, first I need to exercise trust that my Heavenly Father knows my needs and "all flesh is in

---

[14] *Doctrine and Covenants 122:5*
[15] *Doctrine and Covenants 122:6*
[16] *Doctrine and Covenants 122:7*
[17] *Doctrine and Covenants 122:9*
[18] *Doctrine and Covenants 122:9*
[19] *Doctrine and Covenants 123:17*

[His] hands."[20] Because I have this trust, I can therefore act in faith and do those things that will help me productively face my challenges. Rather than grumbling, whining, and wallowing in self-pity, I can choose to "hold on my way," "fear not," and do my part to serve my Heavenly Father and His children. If I do so with a positive outlook, taking time to be still, and have faith, the Lord's plan for me will be revealed. I can also hold on to the firm belief that in His infinite wisdom, Heavenly Father is giving me exactly the experiences that I need for my good. A study of the scriptures reveal that others, including the most elect, have had similar experiences.

THE PSALM OF NEPHI

As I contemplated this powerful lesson, it struck me that just like Joseph Smith, the Book of Mormon prophet Nephi had a similar **if, know, therefore** experience, perhaps rooted in some worry and self-doubt. In 2 Nephi chapter four, what has become known as the Psalm of Nephi, he exclaims, "O wretched man that I am! Yea, my heart sorroweth because of my flesh; my soul grieveth because of mine iniquities."[21] Nephi had a painfully soul-searching **if** moment. Yet he reminded himself of what he knew when he said, "I **know** in whom I have trusted. My God hath been my support; he hath led me through mine afflictions in the wilderness; and he hath preserved me."[22] So rather than wallowing in self-pity, Nephi figuratively dusts himself off and rallies with a few **therefores**, including:

> Awake, my soul! No longer droop in sin. Rejoice, O my heart, and give place no more for the enemy of my soul. Do not anger again because of mine enemies. Do not slacken my strength because of mine afflictions. Rejoice, O my heart, and cry unto the Lord, and say: O Lord, I will praise thee forever; yea, my soul will rejoice in thee, my God, and the rock of my salvation.[23]

ALMA AND AMULON

The Book of Mormon provides another wonderful example of a prophet

---

[20] *Doctrine and Covenants 101:16*
[21] *2 Nephi: 4:17*
[22] *2 Nephi: 4:19–20*
[23] *2 Nephi 4:28–30*

and his people who had to "just hold on" for a season, enduring some very challenging circumstances. In Mosiah chapter twenty-three verse twenty, we read that Alma and his followers "did multiply and prosper exceedingly in the land." However, in verse twenty-one, we learn that "the Lord seeth fit to chasten his people; yea, he trieth their patience and their faith." The trial came as a result of these true followers of the Savior and a very blessed people being brought into bondage by the Lamanites under the leadership of the former wicked priest of Noah, Amulon. Ironically, Alma and his peaceable followers gave themselves up and even promised to show Amulon the way to the Land of Nephi in exchange for liberty. In the end, their hope of freedom was crushed.

As with the Prophet Joseph Smith, Alma and his people were about to experience several challenging **ifs** in spite of the wonderful blessings they had been given as a result of being righteous. As he abridged the record, Mormon recorded that the people would witness a powerful **know**, saying that "none could deliver them but the Lord their God, yea even the God of Abraham and Isaac, and Jacob."[24]

In Mosiah chapter twenty-four, we learn that "Amulon began to exercise authority over Alma and his brethren, and began to persecute him and cause that his children should persecute their children."[25] As a result, "so great were their afflictions that they began to cry mightily to God." As with most faithful who face trials, Alma and his followers practiced the most basic **therefore**; they turned to prayer. Sadly, their captors brought down a drastic **if**, threatening that any "found calling upon God should be put to death."[26] As a testament to their faith, "Alma and his people did not raise their voices to the Lord their God, but did pour out their hearts to Him; and he did know the thoughts of their hearts."[27] Because of their patience and faith, the voice of the Lord came to Alma saying:

> Lift up your heads and be of good comfort, for I know of the covenant which ye have made unto me; and I will . . . deliver them out of bondage. And I will ease their burdens which are put on their

[24] *Alma 23:23*
[25] *Alma 24:8*
[26] *Mosiah 24:11*
[27] *Mosiah 24:12*

shoulders, that even they cannot feel them on your backs, even while you are in bondage; and this will I do that ye may stand as a witness for me hereafter, and that ye may know of a surety that I the Lord God do visit my people in their afflictions.[28]

Just like the revelation given to the Prophet Joseph Smith in Liberty Jail, Heavenly Father pronounced a clear **know** when he proclaimed they would "know of a surety" He would visit His people "in their afflictions."

With that assurance, the people did "submit cheerfully and with patience to all the will of the Lord."[29] As a result, the people were strengthened, and "they did bear up their burdens with ease." However, the burdens were not lifted. Because they did **know** God and **therefore** cried unto Him with patience and faith, they were comforted, bolstered, and delivered out of bondage. After their divinely assisted escape, "They poured out their thanks to God because He had been merciful unto them, and eased their burdens, and had delivered them out of bondage . . . and none could deliver them except it were the Lord their God."[30]

What can we then learn from Nephi, Alma, and Joseph Smith? I believe it is this; even the most righteous will have hard times—the **ifs** of life. Some reasons are to test us, to help us develop patience and faith, and, in the end, for us to "know of a surety" that "God will visit His people." After the hard times, which hopefully turn our hearts and minds to heaven, our journey will be enhanced if we **therefore** take positive principle-based actions.

If, know, therefore is a valuable lesson and a good model for overcoming trials, including those brought on or amplified by worry and anxiety. It is possible to incorporate principles of modern therapies, particularly mindfulness and ACT, into this pattern exemplified by the Prophet Joseph Smith, Nephi, and Alma.

Take just a few moments and consider some of the very significant **ifs** you have endured and hopefully overcome. Perhaps there is a worrisome and anxiety-producing challenge you're facing at this very moment.

---

[28] *Mosiah 24: 13–14*
[29] *Mosiah 24:15*
[30] *Mosiah 24:21*

In the space below list these significant life events with a short description. Briefly describe the **if** and then record the **therefores** you tried. For example, soon after my brother's death from brain cancer, I experienced my first panic attack. Initially, my **therefores** included a lot of research online about anxiety and quick fix remedies. I tried several solutions but, in my impatience, I stuck with none and suffered. Thankfully, I discovered mindfulness, meditation, and ACT, which we will explore later in this book. This activity of recording some of your life's challenges and reflecting on your responses will provide a framework that will help as we introduce more effective tools for dealing with anxiety and stress.

Event 1 (description and summary of how you responded):

Event 2 (description and summary of how you responded):

Event 3 (description and summary of how you responded):

Points to Ponder: There are few guarantees in life, but one we can count on is this: we will have hard times. However, the restored gospel of Jesus Christ provides a sure knowledge that God is in charge and that He gives us experiences for our good, to help us grow and become all that He wants us to become. He also provides the way for us to overcome and grow if we will but trust in Him and take positive actions in accordance to His will.

Questions to Consider: Am I ready to face my fears with positive actions following the pattern of **if, know, therefore?** If not, what is holding me back?

Notes, thoughts, resolutions . . .

"The best antidote for worry is work. The best medicine for despair is service. The best cure for weariness is to help someone even more tired."
—Gordon B. Hinckley

CHAPTER 2

INTRODUCING ACCEPTANCE COMMITMENT THERAPY (ACT)

While Acceptance Commitment Therapy (ACT) is a relatively new treatment, the value of acceptance has been around for some time. In his book "The Road Less Traveled" (1978), M. Scott Peck states:

> Life is difficult. This is a great truth, one of the greatest truths. It is a great truth because once we truly see this truth, we transcend it. Once we truly know that life is difficult—once we truly understand and **accept** it—then life is no longer difficult. Because once it is **accepted**, the fact that life is difficult no longer matters (emphasis added).[31]

"The Serenity Prayer," first published by Reinhold Niebuhr in 1951, is a central part of the twelve-step program for Alcoholics Anonymous. It reminds us of the value of acceptance stating, "God, grant me the serenity to **accept** the things I cannot change, the courage to change the things I can, and the wisdom to know the difference" (emphasis added).

One of the goals of ACT is to help one achieve psychological flexibility through a combination of mindfulness, values, and action.[32] This is illustrated in the equation below:

$$\text{Mindfulness} + \text{Values} + \text{Action} = \text{Psychological Flexibility}$$

Mindfulness is a mental state of awareness with a focus on the present. Values are the reason why we do things. Action is associated with agency and choice.

While ACT does stand for Acceptance Commitment Therapy, the acronym has a second meaning:

---

[31] *Peck, M. Scott. The Road Less Traveled*
[32] *Harris, Russ. The Happiness Trap*

A = Accept Thoughts

C = Choose Values

T = Take Action

The central key to ACT, which runs counter to traditional treatments for anxiety, is to accept your anxious thoughts and feelings. Forsyth and Eifert call these WAFs: short for worries, anxieties, and fears. They argue that rather than the classic cognitive behavioral therapies that focus on managing and getting rid of anxiety; a healthier approach is looking at our thoughts and feelings as friends instead of enemies. Perhaps it is the extraordinary efforts we take to avoid negative thoughts, worry, and pain that become the root of our suffering.

Russ Harris states, "The more we try to find happiness, the more we suffer."[33] In short, the combination of the avoidance of pain with the obsessive pursuit of happiness creates a trap that results in our suffering. Does this mean happiness is bad or should not be sought after? On the contrary, we should want to be happy, but we often have an unrealistic hope that we should rarely be sad, worried, or anxious.

Have you fallen into the traps that come with avoidance and pursuing happiness? Ask yourself this question: What are the worrisome thoughts or anxious feelings I would most like to get rid of?

It is very probable that you, like others, have tried several common remedies in your struggles with worries, anxieties, and fears. Perhaps, you have looked for an "easy button,"—some quick fixes that will make the pain go away. These could include things like counseling, medicine, natural remedies, exercise, drugs, alcohol, avoidance, venting to friends, self-

---

[33] *Harris, Russ. The Happiness Trap*

LESSONS FROM LIBERTY JAIL WITH MINDFULNESS THERAPIES

criticizing, social-media therapy, and more.

What have you tried? Make a list (left column of the box below) of all of the activities, remedies, and therapies, or even things you have avoided, so you would not have these thoughts or feelings. Once you have completed the list, rank the activities from top to bottom in the right column, with the first one being the most effective. If you are like most, you will realize many of your efforts provide only temporary relief.

Remedies Tried	Ranking of Effectiveness

The good news is that ACT has proven to be an effective remedy for overcoming anxiety and fear. When we add the divine lessons from Liberty Jail, healing can be complete and enduring.

ACT – AN ANTIDOTE FOR FEAR

ACT has six principles to help us combat fear, which Hayes uses as an acronym (FEAR) to describe the fusion of thoughts, evaluating experiences, avoidance, and making reasons (justifications) for behavior. Below the steps for FEAR are further explained:

F = Fusion with Thoughts, Images, and Memories:
All of us can become tangled or hooked by our thoughts. When we fuse with our thoughts, we treat them as if they were real and not just imagined. However, thoughts are just words, or as Harris describes, stories in our heads. For example, "panic" is just a word, and the evaluation of panic as "bad" is just a judgment. Forsyth and Eifert describe this as "the mind

trap" that happens "when you go beyond seeing words as words . . . buying into the illusions your mind creates. The thoughts shift from being thoughts to something dangerously serious."[34] This happens when we begin to believe the thoughts are real and not just fictional storylines of our imagination. Fusion happens when we respond to these fictitious storylines as if they are real. This is usually followed by judgments and actions trying to relieve the resulting feelings of anxiety, nervousness, and even panic. Our natural reactive response is to take efforts, sometimes extraordinary, to get rid of those uncomfortable sensations, wanting relief to come instantly.

E = Evaluating Your Experience:
Almost all of our experiences and activities are labeled with some sort of evaluation: good or bad, happy or sad, right or wrong. Remember, these evaluations are judgments, not reality. Like fusion with our thoughts, evaluating an experience may result in suffering of some fashion, and we will be motivated to act on that judgment—again to find relief.

A = Avoiding Your Experiences:
The most common solution for pain resulting from our fusion with negative thoughts is avoidance. Why do we practice avoidance? It often works and brings "a brief honeymoon from the pain and its source."[35] This brief respite from anxiety only fuels further avoidance and escape behavior. Sometimes avoidance is valid, especially if the situation is real—not imagined—and could pose a legitimate threat. However, many of our fears are truly just imaginary worries; thus, avoidance is unnecessary and costly.

R = Reason Giving for Your Behavior:
Reason giving is our rationalization and justification of our actions and beliefs, resulting from the steps of fusion, evaluation, and avoidance. These are the labels we give ourselves; they are the autobiographical titles that describe our often negative and incorrect self-perceptions. The reasons could sound very much like, "I could if I didn't get so nervous when I_____." When we join reason with fear, we become trapped by

---

[34] *Forsyth, John P. and Eifert, Georg H. The Mindfulness and Acceptance Workbook for Anxiety*
[35] *Forsyth, John P. and Eifert, Georg H. The Mindfulness and Acceptance Workbook for Anxiety*

our worries, anxieties, and fears—crippled by "what if" thinking or "I could if only" thoughts.

So what do we do when we have fused with unwanted thoughts and feelings? How can ACT help us cope with the anxiety and fear that come when we have bought into and believed the inaccurate storylines? ACT provides a practical six-step process to combat inaccurate and negative thoughts:

1. **Defusion** is when we learn to think in a new way and not connect (fuse) with the imaginary and false storylines in our minds. Harris states, "As you learn to diffuse painful and unpleasant thoughts, they will lose their ability to frighten, disturb, worry, stress, and depress you."[36]

2. **Expansion** is making room for the unpleasant thoughts and feelings. The official ACT term for this is acceptance. When we accept troublesome thoughts and unpleasant feelings such as anxiety and worry, rather than suppressing them or pushing them away, we are able to overcome these thoughts quickly, resulting in much less suffering.

3. **Connection** is living in the present, moment by moment. This is the essence of mindfulness and disrupts the depressive activity of mourning the past and the anxiety catalyst of worrying about the future.

4. **The Observing Self** is the capacity to stay with troublesome thoughts and feelings, just noticing them and allowing them to come and go without judgment.

5. **Values** are the most empowering part of the ACT therapy. Clarifying and connecting with our values makes life more meaningful. Harris defines values as "reflections of what are most important in your heart: what sort of person you want to be, what is significant and meaningful to you, and what do you want to stand for in life."[37]

---

[36] *Harris, Russ. The Happiness Trap*
[37] *Harris, Russ. The Happiness Trap*

6. **Committed Action** is the last step leading to a more meaningful life, especially if our actions are based on values or the things that matter most.

From a gospel perspective, connecting with our values and taking action are aligned with such eternal principles as divine worth and agency.

Our assertion is that we can combine the simple pattern the Lord provided to the prophet Joseph Smith in Liberty Jail with the proven methods of ACT to promote healing and help "break the chains of worry and anxiety."

The lessons from the scriptures and modern revelation can provide both inspiration and real solutions. We are promised that the Lord can and will heal us because of our faith, good works, and the enabling power of the Atonement. Yet just reading and reciting such phrases as "fear not" and "be still" can only go so far unless we couple those affirmations with action. ACT provides the tools that will make our actions more effective and provide relief and healing.

Points to Ponder: Suffering and anxiety result when we go to great efforts to avoid unpleasant thoughts and feelings. Healing comes when we have the courage to accept these thoughts and feelings, connect with our chosen values, and take action on those things that matter most.

Questions to Consider: What are the things I am avoiding? How could I grow from facing my fears? How have my preoccupations caused me to turn inward or kept me from acting on my values?

Notes, thoughts, resolutions . . .

Notes continued . . .

"I the Lord am bound when you do what I say; but when ye do not what I say, ye have no promise."
—D&C 82:10

CHAPTER 3

PRINCIPLES, PRACTICES, AND PROMISES

The lessons from Liberty Jail provide us with three eternal principles, while ACT offers practical applications with learnable skills that will help us effectively deal with worry and anxiety. The resulting promises are an increased capacity for peace and the eternal assurance that "all these things shall give [me] experience and be for [my] good.[38]"

For example, we know from scripture we will all suffer the effects of the Fall and life will bring us an array of challenges, the "if" moments. As we gain the capacity to accept these challenges with trust, we can have an assurance they will be for our good. This will result in a measure of peace. This assurance is central to the second principle, that we can "know" we are of divine worth. We are His sons and daughters with great capacity and purpose. When we come to know and choose to live by our values, we are blessed with a glorious vision of who we can become. Finally, because of the blessing of agency we can choose to "therefore" act on our values. Taking action on values is the key to both productive living and healing.

When we combine the Lessons from Liberty Jail with ACT and include the principles, practices, and promises, the model looks like this:

IF	KNOW	THEREFORE	
Accept Thoughts	Choose Values	Take Action	FOR MY GOOD
PEACE	VISION	AGENCY	BECOME

In this diagram, the top line represents the principles, the middle the practices, and the bottom the promises. The ultimate promise is that all these experiences, including our struggles with worry, will in the end be for our good, and we will become all the Lord intended for us to become. The final segment includes an arrow symbolizing the becoming process is eternal. The following outline illustrates each principle, with the associated

---

[38] *Doctrine and Covenants 122:7*

practices, and promises:

Principle 1, If: Because of the Fall, all men and women will experience the full spectrum of life, from joy to suffering.

> **Practice 1**: Our capacity to deal with life's challenges improves as we learn to <u>accept thoughts and feelings</u>, living in the present.

> **Promise 1**: As we learn to accept our thoughts and feelings, we will develop greater capacities to "stand still"[39] and have <u>peace</u>.[40]

Principle 2, Know: We are children of God with divine worth and purpose; He gives us experiences for our good, and He will be with us forever and ever.

> **Practice 2**: As we learn to "stand still" and know God, we will understand our divine worth and be inspired to discover our personal vision and <u>choose our values</u>.

> **Promise 2**: An understanding of our divine worth will enable us to create a clear <u>vision</u> of who we are and who we can become.

Principle 3, Therefore: To live up to our full potential and receive all of our foreordained blessings, we must take action.

> **Practice 3**: <u>Taking action</u> is more effective when we have a clear understanding of our goals and the steps to achieve them.

> **Promise 3**: When we take action, we realize the full blessings of <u>agency</u> and the enabling and lifting power of the Atonement.

Over the next few chapters, we will explore in detail these principles and practices. We will also provide exercises and activities to help you gain the skills to mindfully, and with the Lord's help, "overcome all things," including how to break free from poor habits of worry that lead to anxiety. As you proceed, you will be introduced to a simple worksheet that will

---

[39] *Doctrine and Covenants 123:17*
[40] *Doctrine and Covenants 121:7*

guide you through the activities, along with a mindfulness log to record your progress.

> **Points to Ponder:** The Lord has provided eternal principles with associated practices that when followed will result in promised blessings. These principles, practices, and promises are clearly outlined in the revelations given to the prophet Joseph Smith in Liberty Jail.
>
> **Questions to Consider:** As I review my life, how have I personally experienced these principles? What are the practices or remedies I have tried to deal with trials? What have been the results of my efforts to deal with these challenges?

Notes, thoughts, resolutions . . .

Notes continued . .

PRINCIPLE 1, **IF**:

Because of the Fall, all men and women will experience the full spectrum of life, from joy to suffering.

"Here then is a great truth. In the pain, the agony, and the heroic endeavors of life, we pass through a refiner's fire, and the insignificant and the unimportant in our lives can melt away and make our faith bright."
—James E. Faust

CHAPTER 4

IF

IF ⟩ KNOW ⟩ THEREFORE ⟩ FOR MY GOOD ⟩

President Heber J. Grant said, "May we be strengthened with the understanding that being blessed does not mean that we shall always be spared all the disappointments and difficulties of life."

Similarly, the Book of Mormon prophet Lehi counseled his son Jacob in 2 Nephi chapter two that "there must needs be an opposition in all things."[41] He also taught "Adam fell that men might be; and men are, that they might have joy."[42] Without difficulties, we could not comprehend, experience, or even appreciate the good times. Without the Fall, we would not be here. Yet because of the Fall, we became natural men and women, born to experience the full spectrum of life, including the very bad, the wonderfully good, and everything in between. Paradoxically, joy is only possible because we experience sadness.

It is a certainty we will all encounter the **ifs** of life. There will be times of struggle when you and I, like the Prophet Joseph Smith, will look heavenward and ask "Oh God, where art thou? And, where is the pavilion that covereth thy hiding place?"[43]

Regarding the challenges we will all face, President Boyd K. Packer taught:

> We live in a day when the adversary stresses on every hand the philosophy of instant gratification. We seem to demand instant everything, including instant solutions to our problems. We are indoctrinated that somehow we should always be instantly emotionally

---

[41] *2 Nephi 2:11*
[42] *2 Nephi 2:25*
[43] *Doctrine and Covenants 121:1*

comfortable. When that is not so, some become anxious—and all too frequently seek relief from counseling, from analysis, and even from medication. It was meant to be that life would be a challenge. To suffer some anxiety, some depression, some disappointment, even some failure is normal. Teach our members that if they have a good, miserable day once in a while, or several in a row, to stand steady and face them. Things will straighten out. There is great purpose in our struggle in life.[44]

Perhaps President Packer is right regarding our demand and expectation for instant everything, including solutions to eliminate worry and anxiety. Is our modern-day angst a result of dozens, if not hundreds of remedies, all just a quick Internet search away? Consider for a moment what Nephi, Alma, or Joseph Smith could turn to when they had a headache, toothache, persistent worry, or heartache. Surely the options were few and included things like chewing on willow bark, praying, or just toughing it out. They also had the blessing of living with much less noise. They went to bed soon after dark, awakened at first light, read more, worked hard, and actually talked with people face-to-face.

Maybe there is real value in our struggle, as illustrated in the story of the Emperor Moth cited by Forsyth and Eifert in "The Mindfulness and Acceptance Workbook for Anxiety:"[45]

STRUGGLE OF THE EMPEROR MOTH

A biologist found the cocoon of an emperor moth and took it into his lab for study. It sat on his lab table for quite a while. Finally, the cocoon began to tremble as the moth made its efforts to get out into the world.

The scientist noticed that the cocoon was shaped like a bottle: wide at the bottom but very narrow at the top. The top was made of a concrete-like substance. The scientist thought, "There's no way the moth will make it through that hard material."

---

[44] *Ensign May 1978*
[45] *Klemp 1988 cited in Forsyth, John P. and Eifert, Georg H. The Mindfulness and Acceptance Workbook for Anxiety*

He watched the cocoon for a while, getting more and more impatient. Finally he decided to help the moth out. He took a tiny pair of scissors and carefully cut through the hard, concrete-like material, opening the cocoon at the top.

The moth popped out almost instantly. The biologist waited for the moth to spread its beautiful wings and show its pretty colors, but nothing happened. The moth was misshapen, with a huge body and very tiny wings. It finally died, unable to lift itself off the ground.

The scientist began to read about the emperor moth, trying to figure out what had happened. Other people had made the same mistake he had, trying to help the moth into the world. It seems there is a purpose for the moth's cocoon being shaped the way it is.

In order for the moth to fit itself through the narrow neck of the cocoon, it must streamline its body. The fluids in its body are squeezed into the wings, which make them large and the body small. When it finally emerges into the world, the emperor moth is a creature unsurpassed in beauty.

The scientist realized that by trying to spare the moth what he considered unnecessary hardship, he had actually done it a disservice.

Is it possible to look at our trials, struggles, worry, and anxiety in a positive light? Growth comes when we stretch, and sometimes we need a nudge or perhaps a more forceful push to get out of our comfort zone. One of my favorite quotes regarding the value of struggle comes from Elisabeth Kübler-Ross:

> The most beautiful people we have known are those who have known defeat, known suffering, known struggle, known loss, and have found their way out of the depths. These persons have an appreciation, a sensitivity, and an understanding of life that fills them with compassion, gentleness, and a deep loving concern. Beautiful people do not just happen.

Sadly, most of the world does not view adversity, worry, and anxiety from such spiritual perspectives. Elder Orson F. Whitney expresses how to view these negative thoughts from an eternal viewpoint:

> No pain that we suffer, no trial that we experience is wasted. It ministers to our education, to the development of such qualities as patience, faith, fortitude, and humility. All that we suffer and all that we endure, especially when we endure it patiently, builds up our characters, purifies our hearts, expands our souls, and makes us more tender and charitable, more worthy to be called the children of God, and it is through sorrow and suffering, toil and tribulation, that we gain the education that we come here to acquire and which will make us more like our Father and Mother in heaven. [46]

SECULAR VS. SPIRITUAL ORIGINS

People of all eras have had different and unique challenges. Thankfully, all of Heavenly Father's children from the beginning of time are blessed with the Light of Christ. In contrast, there have been and always will be opposing views and alternatives. Some are just options, and other solutions definitely are not in alignment with eternal truths. And sometimes, true principles are hidden behind secular masks.

For example, the secular world argues that we respond automatically to certain situations because we evolved from the sea, at some point became reptiles, and eventually arrived as Neanderthals. Our caveman forefathers had to live each day with two primary motivations: first, to eat and second, not to be some prehistoric creature's lunch. Of course, there were secondary motivations like the company of others, the need to stay warm, and innate urges to continue the species. Our autonomic nervous system drives our unconscious actions of fight-or-flight (sympathetic) and rest-and-digest, feed-and-breed (parasympathetic). We react, live, love, and fear because of the complex interplay of the reptile brain, the limbic system from our mammal ancestors, and our primate legacy, the neo-cortex. As a result, mankind is wired to worry, react (perhaps even overreact), and suffer.

In contrast, eternal and revealed truths teach us that in spite of our

---

[46] *Orson F. Whitney, quoted by Spencer W. Kimball, in "Faith Precedes the Miracle"*

divine origins, we all suffer from the effects of the Fall. Like Adam and Eve, we will have sorrow and experience death (see Genesis 3:17–19). Yet that is part of the purpose of life; without the Fall we could not have obtained our physical bodies, learned from both the good and bad, or developed faith. Learning and growing require the opposition of all things—the good, the bad, and the in-between. Even the Savior experienced the full measure of the Fall. The Book of Mormon prophet Alma described the Savior as:

> Suffering pains and afflictions and temptations of every kind; and this that the word might be fulfilled which saith he will take upon Him the pains and the sicknesses of His people. And he will take upon Him death, that he may loose the bands of death.[47]

The Apostle Paul taught, "Though he were a Son, yet he learned obedience by the things which he suffered."[48] Peter stated, "Christ also suffered for us, leaving us an example, that we should follow his steps."[49] The Savior Himself said:

> For behold, I, God, have suffered these things for all, that they might not suffer if they would repent; But if they would not repent they must suffer even as I; Which suffering caused myself, even God, the greatest of all, to tremble because of pain, and to bleed at every pore, and to suffer both body and spirit—and would that I might not drink the bitter cup, and shrink.[50]

Suffering is part of life and much of it is unavoidable, but what about the pain that is self-inflicted? Perhaps it is because of mistakes, sins committed, poor choices, or bad habits. Often it is because we take great effort to avoid things that cause us worry or pain. At other times we aggressively pursue things that will relieve pain and suffering or bring us temporary happiness. This pursuit will bring an attachment, and "every attachment generates an equally powerful fear that we'll either fail to get what we want or lose

---

[47] *Alma 7:11–12*
[48] *Hebrews 5:8*
[49] *1 Peter 2:21*
[50] *Doctrine and Covenants 19:16–18*

whatever we've already gained. This fear is known as aversion."[51] As we face the trials of life, we will deal with both aversion and attachment, two of life's poisons named by Buddha. Another is ignorance. According to Buddha, these three poisons are the roots of suffering. From a modern perspective, aversion or avoidance would be synonymous with worry and fear. Attachment could be termed obsession. In either case, our attempts at avoidance or attachment can put our life out of balance, a result of a hyper-focus on a particular challenge or frenetic searches for solutions.

The philosopher Aristotle illustrated the importance of a life in balance when he taught the principle of the Golden Mean. His classic examples included putting opposite character traits on each end of a spectrum. The diagram below reviews the two traits of courage and caution:

The Golden Mean

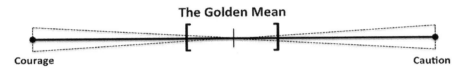

Courage   Caution

In an ancient battle with armies arrayed on a field, there would be one soldier in each army that could receive the designation as the most courageous. On the opposite side, there would be the one that would be the most cautious, afraid, or prone to worry. Once the battle began, neither one of these soldiers would do his side much good. The bravest would charge across the field and take on the biggest, baddest, toughest enemy or enemies and last about a minute. The coward would run, hide, or maybe even desert. Aristotle taught that somewhere in the middle would be an acceptable range: a blend of courage and caution— the Golden Mean. Perhaps, there would be a few with the perfect mix, but the objective was to be within the span of the Golden Mean. Those within this range would be the most effective.

The lesson of the Golden Mean applies very well to aversion and attachment. The following diagram illustrates the need to avoid both extremes and seek balance:

---

[51] *Rinpoche, Yongey Mingyur and Swanson, Eric. The Joy of Living*

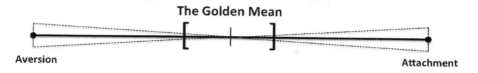

The Golden Mean

Aversion

Attachment

Sometime after my brother's death, I experienced several sleepless nights. For nearly fifty years of my life, I never really struggled with sleep. I actually never gave it much thought. Looking back, even the times we had little babies were easy for me, mostly because of my unselfish wife. As I struggled through this new challenge, I developed a very real aversion or fear of insomnia. I would go to all efforts to not lay awake in bed. I sought out dozens of solutions, including medical sleep aids, natural remedies, ambient sounds, yoga, relaxation techniques, and more. When something seemed to help, it suddenly became an almost obsessive attachment. Thus, I was swinging from one side of the spectrum to the other and making myself miserable.

Thankfully, I discovered ACT and mindfulness, which helped tremendously. There really is something about accepting an anxious moment, facing fears, and putting things in perspective.

Usually, aversion and avoidance issues are easy to spot. We avoid things we don't like, especially things that cause us anxiety, fear, or even panic. Some examples include air travel, public speaking, onstage performances, dogs, and spiders. In contrast, our attachments are more difficult to single out. In my pursuit of reducing anxiety, I started physically exercising more consistently and with real intent. I did this partly because nearly every study on stress management extolled the value of exercise. However, anything done in excess can become an obsession, which can lead to a counter-productive lifestyle. For instance, I discovered my favorite workout was riding my bike, and the best time to ride in Idaho's Upper Snake River Valley is at first light because there is usually no wind. Most days my rides were enjoyable and meditative; I felt much better. However, some mornings I would wake up and a storm would be rolling through, or I would discover my bike had a flat tire. I knew my bike-riding career had moved a bit too far toward an unhealthy attachment when the cancelled ride ruined my attitude and sometimes my day.

Elder Dallin H. Oaks gave a remarkable talk on balance called "Our Strengths Can Become Our Downfall." He stated, "If we are not wary, Satan can cause our spiritual downfall by corrupting us through our strengths as well as by exploiting our weaknesses."[52] He taught that such noble gifts as being led by the spirit, being patriotic, setting goals, and doing family history work could become our downfall if taken to the extreme.

Here is a personal story from the private practice of ACT therapist Dr. Dallas Johnson that illustrates how even being a caring and passionate parent can be out of balance.

Scott's Story

As a teenager, Scott was invited to receive therapy because of a court hearing. The first meetings were with the young man and his parents, who were all Latter-day Saints. Right away, it was obvious that the parent's emotional stability was riding upon Scott's choosing to follow the gospel. Though their intentions were righteous, they had moved from the Golden Mean of lovingly teaching Scott and allowing him to govern himself to an extreme attachment of making absolutely sure he learned the gospel, accepted its teachings, and never made mistakes. They had zero tolerance for exploration, choosing friends, or missing church. Their goal for therapy was to fix Scott so he could fully embrace the gospel. What the parents did not see was that, like the impatient biologist watching the emperor moth, their desire to have him live the gospel perfectly and never make mistakes was preventing Scott from experiencing the beautiful squeezing effect of choice and consequence that would shape his wings of moral development. Sadly, he had become so entrenched with resentment and hatred toward his parents that he became strongly attached to the thought, "If my parents don't want me to do it, then that is exactly what I am going to do." His behavior was not dictated by moral thoughts, but rather through a reaction against the oppression. In this state, neither the parents nor Scott were truly free emotionally or spiritually. They were all slaves to attachment.

---

[52] *Ensign October 1994*

So, what do we do if we sense we are trapped by either avoidance or attachment? What if we sense that our life is out of balance as we strive to avoid pain or obsessively seek remedies? Over the next few chapters, we will review the effective solutions of ACT, shared from a gospel perspective.

Points to Ponder: We will have hard times and face opposition. Our natural tendency is to avoid the resulting suffering or to actively seek solutions. A hyper focus on either avoidance or an attachment to a solution may result in a life out of balance.

Questions to Consider: How "in balance" is my life? What are the activities, passions, pursuits, or perhaps obsessions that can put my life's balance in jeopardy?

Notes, thoughts, resolutions . . .

"Your thoughts are the architects of your destiny."
—David O. McKay

CHAPTER 5

ACCEPT THOUGHTS AND FEELINGS

- - - - - - -

Practice 1: Our capacity to deal with life's challenge improves as we learn to <u>accept thoughts and feelings</u>, living in the present.

IF	KNOW	THEREFORE	
Accept Thoughts			FOR MY GOOD
PEACE			

When life happens, positive or negative, we almost always make judgments. In the Liberty Jail revelations, you can sense the pain and justified anger the Prophet Joseph Smith was feeling toward the enemies of the Church. There is a real sense that for a season he felt very much alone, almost forgotten by the Lord. While it is impossible to analyze his worries, anxiety, and fears, they had to be very real.

Just like the prophet and Liberty Jail, our challenging life events may be followed by thoughts, worries, and fear. Our ruminations are almost always followed by anxious feelings. This then leads to aversion, attachment, and suffering. Over time, our accumulation of thoughts results in the lens through which we see the world. A Vietnam combat veteran said, "Thoughts are the serpents that slither up our spines. You've got yours, and I've got mine. First we can't think, and then we can't feel; because we're too busy thinking our thoughts are real."

PERCEPTIONS AND PARADIGMS

Perceptions and paradigms are tricky but so powerful. We see the world not as it is but as we are. In my freshman psychology class, I first learned about the power of awareness or perception. We become more aware of things that directly impact us or are top-of-mind. For example, one of my first car purchases was an AMC Gremlin, which had a very unique name and body style. Very few would call the Gremlin a classy, good-looking vehicle. In fact, it was so unique that its design alone was very noticeable. I never really paid attention to the Gremlin. However, once I owned one, I noticed them everywhere. Did they suddenly become a very popular car? No. My awareness and perception changed. When we are dealing with troublesome issues, our awareness, perceptions, and paradigms will certainly be affected, often in negative ways. Those things we focus on or worry about can and often will be amplified. It is often said, "that which we resist, persists."

Here is an example of a young lady Dr. Dallas Johnson helped. She had developed a real negative paradigm: a phobia of snakes.

Sally's Story

Sally had a snake phobia. Terror, true horror, and fright would course through her body whenever she thought about, saw, or even heard the word snake. Most people would not notice how ubiquitous images of snakes are, because unless a snake is actually wrapped around their body, their mind is not attuned to them. However, Sally's mind was like a well-trained bird dog, looking to sniff out and sharply point out anything that remotely resembled or reminded her of a snake. She could literally tell you every place in the area that she could find pictures, stuffed animals, or replicas of snakes because she lived in terror of them. So, the lens through which she saw the world had a built-in radar for snakes. Her awareness and perception caused her see danger (in the form of snakes) everywhere.

BLIND SPOTS

Another term in psychology is "scotomas" or, simply defined, our blind spots. We all have them. Here is an experiment. If you live in the United States, ask someone, "How many countries have the 4th of July?" The answer is almost always one. What is the correct answer? Every country that uses the Greco Roman Calendar has the 4th of July. However, Americans almost automatically conclude July 4th belongs exclusively to the United States.

Sometimes we can even artificially and temporarily create blind spots or alter perceptions. Here are two fun experiments. Invite someone to say "spot" out loud ten times, and then ask, "What do you do when you come to a green light?" The most common, almost automatic response is "stop!" A similar game is to ask someone to say "ten" ten times, and then ask, "What is an aluminum can made from?" The answer is usually "tin."

How are blind spots, or false beliefs and perceptions, formed? Dr. Maxwell Malz in "Psycho-cybernetics" and Dr. Bobbe Sommer in the companion piece "Psycho-cybernetics 2000" explore how our beliefs, especially inaccurate perceptions, are formed and how they affect our lives. Dr. Sommer states, "Every one of us always acts, feels, and behaves in a manner that is consistent with our self-image, regardless of the reality of that image."[53] Often, these beliefs are formed very early in our lives and are by–products of many life events. Our beliefs, perceptions, and even our self-images are products of an interesting interchange between the left and right parts of our brains. While recent findings have found both sides of the brain are often active, this simplistic model provides valid insights on how learning and perceptions are formed.

LEFT BRAIN / RIGHT BRAIN

The left side of our brains could be given the label "the rational brain." This hemisphere is very analytical, structural, and is where we often learn things first—usually by following written or verbal instructions. In contrast, the right side is "the intuitive brain." It likes images: it is imaginative and creative. Learning here happens by observation. Often, things are learned in the left-brain first, but once they become instinctive, the right-brain takes over.

---

[53] Sommer, Bobbe. *Psycho-cybernetics 2000*

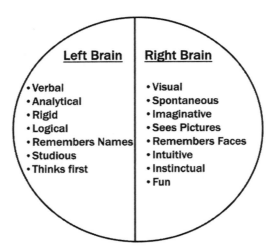

Dr. Malz used the example of learning to tie shoes. At first, it is very verbal with step-by-step instructions. Overtime, with patience, practice, and repetition, this activity becomes habit and is accomplished with little or no thought. You can apply this to many activities, like driving a car, keyboarding, or playing the piano. When driving a car, have you ever caught yourself wondering, "How did I get here?" You certainly did dozens of activities, like watching and reacting to traffic flow, turning on your blinker, changing lanes, switching radio stations, and turning on and off the windshield wipers, all with no real conscious thought. This would be in stark contrast to the days when you first learned to drive a car.

Dr. Sommer expanded on these principles by identifying factors governing each side of the brain. First, the left "rational brain" is governed by the principles "select and eliminate." In contrast, the right "intuitive brain" lives by "agree and comply."

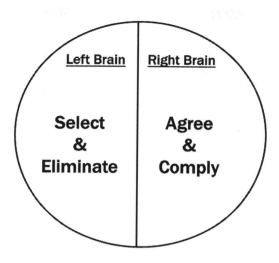

For instance, when you go to a restaurant and look at the menu, the left-brain immediately gets involved. First, you analyze all of the options. This may take some time, even a bit of internal debate. Once the analysis is over, a selection is made, and all other options are eliminated. Once you choose beef steak, chicken is off the board. Now the intuitive brain comes into play: it agrees and complies, very much looking forward to steak.

Sometimes this interplay affects our emotional and physical states. One day I arrived at work, and a colleague said, "You don't look like you are feeling well." Interestingly, up until that very moment I was feeling just fine. Well, that was until the left-brain started analyzing, reviewing, and contemplating that perhaps I was sick. If I was not very careful, the troublesome debate would lead my rational self to select "yep, I'm sick," which eliminated "I'm well." Then the right side just agreed and complied, and I actually started feeling poorly.

As we consider our self-image, the dynamics of our left and right brains plays a major role in how our paradigms are formed. Our parents, teachers, coaches, and friends have unwittingly shaped our beliefs because of the select/eliminate and agree/comply process. Sometimes the results are very constructive resulting in positive self-image and personal expectation. In contrast, negative labels or criticism can damage our self-esteem and outlook.

Christopher's Story

Christopher had developed a real fear of singing in public. When someone asked, "What's up? I know you can sing, why don't you try?" he recounted a time he sang at a public program where his family was the entertainment. He was about ten years old and had one solo. He didn't mention any compliments, but he did share one perceived negative review from a friend of the family who said, "You sing like a girl." Well, he very much wanted to sing like a man and bottled this up, and every time he remembered that comment, his left-brain selected "sings like a girl" and eliminated "could sing like a man." Each time he fretted and worried he would be asked to sing in the future, the left-brain played the same game. And of course, the right-brain just agreed and complied. His perception and scotoma was that he would always sing like a female. Yet a true perception was that most ten-year-old boys sing like girls, but most will grow out of their soprano youth. Interestingly, grown men who retain the capacity to hit those countertenor high notes are usually the stars of the show.

Regardless of how our beliefs were formed, they impact how we think, feel, and act. For example, Christopher's false self-image of his perceived incapacity to sing impacted how he felt and performed, which lead to several aversion and attachment extremes. To this day, he will likely do all he can to avoid singing in public. The sad fact is his blind spot is inaccurate; a false perception compounded by worry and associated feelings of anxiety.

Dr. Martin Rossman stated in his book "The Worry Solution" that the "discrepancy between the real and imagined is the root of suffering." The following graphic illustrates how this discrepancy can lead to anxiety and/or depression.

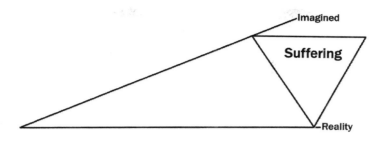

The larger the gap between our worried or imagined self and our real self, the more suffering we will experience and endure. Let's use the example of the ten-year-old male soprano as a case study. In reality, he had great capacity and potential as a singer. Yet, because of his worry and fear, his imagined self was way off target, and that gap resulted in fear, anxiety, worry, and suffering. The opportunity and challenge is to come to an accurate and correct perception of our real self. In reality, it really does start and end with how we think.

So, if thinking is part of the problem, how do we deal with our worrisome thoughts? One approach is to follow several of the classic Cognitive Behavior Therapies designed to help us change our thinking by combating negative thought patterns with a goal to change our self-image or perception.

For example, in "Psycho-cybernetics 2000," Dr. Sommer offers a simple solution to help us cancel negative thoughts and attend to those more positive. The process is outlined in the acronym CRAFT:

C = Cancel all negative thoughts like "I can't sing."

R = Replace each negative thought with a positive one like "I am a great singer."

A = Affirm out loud several times the positive statement "I am a great singer."

F = Focus or visualize success (in this instance, singing well).

T = Train or "act as if" you have already arrived at being a very good singer.

After my first reading of "Psycho-cybernetics 2000," I became an avid believer in CRAFT and saw some positive results with this classic Cognitive Behavior Therapy. Yet I was always bothered that in my practice I was even more focused on my thoughts, becoming more attached to any positive thought and sometimes more tuned into my fears. Too often, my relief was temporary.

However, with ACT we learn that it is not the imagination that is the problem, but rather how much we buy into or believe the imagined thing or worry that causes suffering. Perhaps Dr. Rossman is using the word "imagined" to mean something that we believe strongly. There is nothing inherently dangerous about what our minds produce; what matters is what we attend to. I can think "I'm an idiot" and at the same time think "I'm a valued son/daughter of God," and the one I attend to is the one that will have more influence over my emotions and behaviors. I do not have to get rid of unwanted thoughts in order to attend to helpful thoughts. ACT provides very good tools on dealing with unwanted and troublesome thoughts, yet I believe can be more effective than traditional Cognitive Behavior Therapy because it avoids the struggle of combating thoughts and changing perceptions. For me personally, the practices of acceptance, connecting with values, and taking positive actions have provided more positive and permanent results.

Over the next three chapters, we will explore in detail the exercises that support the practice of acceptance, which will increase your capacity to "stand still."[54] This will enable you to deal more productively with unwanted thoughts and feelings, while at the same time giving you the tools to take effective value-based action.

---

[54] *Doctrine and Covenants 123:17*

Points to Ponder: Perception is reality, even when your beliefs or paradigms are inaccurate due to your life experiences. The larger the gap between your real self and your imagined negative false perceptions, the more you will suffer.

Questions to Consider: What are my false perceptions that may be holding me back? How am I negatively affected by personal blind spots that are the results of fear or worry?

Notes, thoughts, resolutions . . .

"Between stimulus and response, there is a space. In that space is our power to choose our response. In our response lies our growth and our freedom."
—Viktor Frankl

CHAPTER 6

MIND THE GAP

- - - - - - -

ACCEPTANCE Exercise 1

A few years ago, I had the privilege of traveling to London with my daughter. As we traveled around the city, we used their subway system, the Tube. The phrase "mind the gap" was broadcast almost constantly over intercoms and posted on signs everywhere. Why? Between the loading platform and the train cars was a fairly significant gap of around four to six inches. The space was large enough that if people were not careful, they could slip, getting their feet, ankles, or even legs caught. The results could be a tragic injury or worse. For me, "mind the gap" is a good reminder to take time to be still and make space or a gap between life's events and my responses. Creating this space helps me stop the worry cycle, allowing me to listen for promptings and to choose to act according to my values.

BETWEEN STIMULUS AND RESPONSE

In her book "Taking the Leap," Pema Chodron shares the story of her friend giving her a bone shaped pendant that, instead of a dog's name, said, "Sit, Stay, Heal." [55]

She believes we can find healing in these three simple words. Human tendencies are to react to unpleasant circumstances in such habitual ways as fear, anxiety, or anger. Instead, "sit, stay, heal" reminded her to take time to

---

[55] *Chodron, Pema. Taking the Leap*

meditate, to be present, and to heal. This is done through mindfulness and meditation, which helps create a gap or space between stimulus and response. She stated, "When we pause, we naturally know what to do. We begin, due to our own wisdom, to move toward letting go and fearlessness."[56] By creating space and listening to our inner wisdom, we will intuitively make better choices with more proactive responses. This is in contrast to the typical stimulus/response model. Simply put, things happen and we react, just like touching your hand on a hot stove. Sometimes the stimulus is our thoughts, like imagination or worry. In a reactive model, our responses are based on aversion, attachment, or both (see diagram below):

Chodron teaches us that mindfulness and meditation allow us to create some space between stimulus and response. It is between this gap, (see diagram below) where our natural intuition or "inner wisdom" can enable us to respond in more positive ways.

From a gospel perspective, this gap can allow for so much more than just our intuition and inner wisdom. First, there is agency, what Stephen R. Covey called our "freedom to choose," based on our self-awareness, imagination, conscience, and independent will. It is in this gap (see the diagram on the next page) where we can be most receptive to the whisperings of the Holy Ghost, where the enabling power of the Atonement will give us the strength to make right choices – choices based on our core values, guided by heaven.

---

[56] *Chodron, Pema. Taking the Leap*

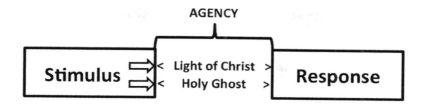

As I read the works of Chodron and other meditation scholars, I believe they are mostly right. However, I prefer a different terminology using the same principles. Our inner wisdom, intuition, and conscience are just synonyms for the Light of Christ. In Moroni Chapter seven, verse sixteen we read:

> For behold, the Spirit of Christ is given to every man, that he may know good from evil; wherefore, I show unto you the way to judge; for every thing which inviteth to do good, and to persuade to believe in Christ, is sent forth by the power and gift of Christ; wherefore ye may know with a perfect knowledge it is of God.[57]

Many reading this book will also enjoy the added blessing of having the Holy Ghost provide inspiration and direction within the gap we create through mindfulness and meditation. We have many opportunities to "stand still" and make space for this inspiration to come as we participate in the sacrament and serve in holy temples. Since almost all worry is based on inaccurate beliefs, the promptings from the Light of Christ and the Holy Ghost will help put thoughts in true perspective.

Given our very busy world, our digital age, and the tendency to be plugged in, there has never been a greater need to take time to "stand still."[58] Elder M. Russell Ballard taught:

> It is important to be still and listen and follow the Spirit. We simply have too many distractions to capture our attention, unlike any time in the history of the world.

> Everyone needs time to meditate and contemplate. Even the Savior of the world, during His mortal ministry, found time to do so: "And

---

[57] *Moroni 7:16*
[58] *Doctrine and Covenants 123:17*

when he had sent the multitudes away, he went up into a mountain apart to pray: and when the evening was come, he was there alone."

We all need time to ask ourselves questions or to have a regular personal interview with ourselves. We are often so busy and the world is so loud that it is difficult to hear the heavenly words "be still, and know that I am God."[59]

For "mind the gap" there is one activity I have given the name STA²R (with the "A" squared). This activity provides a basic introduction to acceptance:

1. **S**top and recognize unpleasant thoughts (worries) and feelings (anxiety).
2. **T**ake a deep breath, beginning with one deep breath followed by another.
3. **A**ccept things as they are, including thoughts and feelings, with caring, curiosity, and understanding.
4. **A**sk yourself what you really want, taking into consideration your values.
5. **R**eact in a positive way in alignment with your values and true to your vision.

The STA²R activity is illustrated in the following diagram:

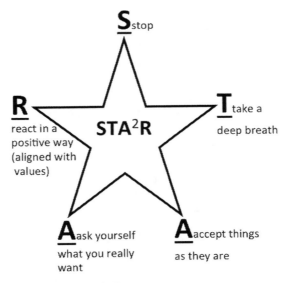

S stop

R react in a positive way (aligned with values)

T take a deep breath

STA²R

A ask yourself what you really want

A accept things as they are

---

[59] *CES Devotional, "Be Still and Know that I am God," May 2014*

The next time you have the urge to react, perhaps in a negative way, consciously make the choice to pause and practice STA²R. To make this activity a habit, take time each day to practice these steps. Over time, you will catch yourself "minding the gap" and responding in proactive ways in alignment with your values.

I am confident this activity and those you will learn in the following chapters will increase your capacity to be still and to know not only God[60] but also who you are and the things that should matter most in your life— your personal mission (vision) and values. When you stand still, you have the added blessing of "see[ing] the salvation of God and for His arm to be revealed." [61]

> **Points to Ponder:** When we develop the capacity to create a gap between stimulus and response, we become more open to feelings and promptings from both the Light of Christ and the Holy Ghost. It is in this gap that we can benefit most from the enabling power of the Atonement.
>
> **Questions to Consider:** Do I regularly take time to just be still? How would I be blessed if I increased my capacity to pause and not respond in a reactive way?

Notes, thoughts, resolutions . . .

---

[60] *Doctrine and Covenants 101:16*
[61] *Doctrine and Covenants 123:17*

"Patience means accepting that which
cannot be changed and facing
it with courage, grace, and faith."
–Dieter F. Uchtdorf

CHAPTER 7

Accept

- - - - - - -

ACCEPTANCE Exercise 2

It is my belief that the Prophet Joseph Smith did not passively resign himself to his fate. He faced the challenges of Liberty Jail with patience, courage, grace, and faith. He waited on the Lord with trust and acceptance.

We can follow his example and learn to accept our trials, fears, worries, and anxieties. A good first step is creating a gap between stimulus and response, but we still have to deal with the troublesome thoughts that may want to occupy that space. Fortunately, ACT provides several solutions that are effective in helping us not fuse with unwanted thoughts and worries. Plus, we have the added assurances that we can and will receive divine help. Each of these have merit. Depending on your individual personality, one or more may be ideally suited for you. The key is to pick one and practice it consistently for some time. Once you become skilled at the activity and it becomes instinctual (right-brain), consider adding a second or third skill to your arsenal. If one mindfulness activity is enough to move you off of worry, have a mini-celebration, but don't stop practicing!

In "The Happiness Trap," Dr. Russ Harris says that an important step in ACT is to not connect or fuse with negative thoughts. The mindfulness activity of just noticing the thought and letting it go naturally is effective. The suggestion is to just give the thought a label, like "there is worry," and then gently move off the thought, letting it go. One suggestion is to give a recurring thought a name and then call that thought by name and just let it pass. For example, I gave a particular worry the name "Knucklehead." When the thought showed up I would just say, "hello Knucklehead" and give it a brief wink and smile. I then returned to whatever I was doing. I soon noticed that while early on Knucklehead would show up often throughout the day, it soon became a more infrequent guest.

In one of my first mindfulness workshops, meditation scholar Dr. Gary Purse likened our mind to a pasture and our thoughts to a horse. Picture in your mind a beautiful pasture with lush green grass. Quite suddenly galloping into this pasture is a horse. Let's say this horse represents a troublesome thought or worry. With this horse, we have three choices. First, and most instinctive, is to try and chase the horse away. We can yell at the horse, chase after it with a stick, or perhaps throw stones. Yet the harder we try, the more persistently the horse will just run around the pasture. The longer we chase, the more stubborn and annoying the horse becomes. Consequently, the horse, or in this case the unwanted thought, will just persist and amplify. The second choice is to try and catch the horse, perhaps tie it up, and put on a saddle followed by a bridle. If you try to break this annoying thought like you would a bucking bronco, the results will be similar to your efforts of chasing the thought away. The final and best option is to just acknowledge the horse. You could even give it a nod, but then just let it be. In most cases, the horse may hang around for a while, but will soon leave on its own accord. In the meantime, while the horse is wandering around your pasture, you keep busy taking care of the things you value, thus defusing the worrisome thought.

In essence, when we defuse a thought by acceptance, we don't actively select it, thus disrupting the select/eliminate and agree/comply sequence. The worry, anxiety, or fear has no hold on us.

This is in contrast to some of my early strategies in conquering worry. I've tried singing hymns, memorizing scripture, reciting inspirational quotes, and even snapping my wrist with a rubber band (it hurts). All of these have merit when dealing with troublesome thoughts, fears, and worries, but most focus on avoidance (chasing the horse) or attachment (riding the horse) and for me proved to be ineffective.

The central activity of defusing thoughts is a simple mindful meditation focusing on the breath, which most meditation experts recommend as a good first step. Mindful breathing slows down and may eventually interrupt the automatic responses from our sympathetic nervous system: the classic fight or flight response. This increases our capacity to be still and not attach to unwanted thoughts and feelings.

Note: You will find at the back of the book the Mindfulness Activity Log. As you begin these activities, please record your efforts and thoughts. Consistent practice is key to success. You can also download a copy at https://lessonsfromlibertyjail.com.

Acceptance Activity 1: Defusion with Mindful Breathing[62]

Start by getting comfortable in a place where you'll be undisturbed for five to ten minutes or so. You may sit on the floor or in a chair. Sit upright with your palms up or down on your lap.

Close your eyes and gently guide your attention to the natural rhythm of your breath in your chest and belly. Simply notice the breath as you breathe in . . . and out . . . in . . . and out. There's no need to make the breath slower, deeper, or shallower. Just allow your breathing to do its thing. Sense the air passing from the chest through your nose and mouth as you breathe in . . . and out.

Continue to notice your breathing with a sense of kindness and gentle allowance. There's nothing to do except notice your breath. Sink into its natural rhythm: the rising and gentle falling of your chest and belly as you breathe in and out . . . in and out.

When you find your mind wandering (and you will), or if you feel distracted, just kindly notice it and return your attention to the rhythm of your breath and the rising and falling of your chest and belly. Continue this activity of kind observation for as long as you wish—just notice your breath doing its thing.

Then, when you are ready, gradually widen your attention, and gently open your eyes with the intention of bringing this skill of kind observation to your experience throughout the day.

The more you practice, the better you will become at living in the moment, coming back to your present experience, noticing troublesome thoughts (horses in the pasture), and not connecting or fusing with them.

---

[62] *Adapted from "The Mindfulness and Acceptance Workbook for Anxiety;" Forsyth and Eifert 2008*

As with all mindfulness tools, the key is practice. One of my students (a meditation fan) stated, "Practice is a success. If my mind wanders a hundred times during a five-minute practice, it's not that I failed a hundred times. If I am able to practice redirecting my mind a hundred times, when the real experiences come along, my mind will have practiced redirecting itself."

The practice of meditative breathing will also increase your capacity to "stand still" and create space. The second activity, observing, will help with acceptance.

. . . .

Acceptance Activity 2: Observing

The key to this option is to observe your thoughts and not react to worry, anxiety, or fear. This takes a bit of patience and some courage, because your initial urge will be to cut-and-run (aversion) and/or to dash for some remedy (attachment). Observing helps you develop the skill of sitting or staying with the uncomfortable thought or emotion and just letting it pass. This is like the Lord's advice to Joseph Smith to "therefore hold on."[63] All emotions have a shelf life, and if you don't fuse with or attach to the emotion, you will be surprised with just how short it will last. If you try and chase it away, or put the saddle on, be prepared for an extended journey. Forsyth and Eifert[64] called their observation activity "mind watching," and the following is adapted from their workbook to fit our horse and pasture theme.

Get in a comfortable place where you won't be disturbed. Begin by taking a series of slow, deep breaths. Keep this up through the entire practice. Imagine your mind is a pasture, with a front gate and a back gate. Thoughts can enter in or leave from either gate. Pay attention to each thought (the horse) as it enters.

Watch the thought until it leaves. Don't try to analyze or hold on to it. Just acknowledge having the thought. It is only a moment in your mind, a brief visitor to your pasture. If you start judging yourself for having the

---

[63] *Doctrine and Covenants 122:9*
[64] *Forsyth, John P. and Eifert, Georg H. The Mindfulness and Acceptance Workbook for Anxiety*

thought, then notice that. Don't argue with your mind's judgment. Simply notice it and give it a label: "judging" or "worry." For example, "There's judging" or "There's worry." Some thoughts won't be negative at all, and you could label them "planning" or "daydreaming." The key to this activity is to notice thoughts rather than fusing with them. How will you know if you are getting caught up? Usually by your emotional reactions and how long each horse (thought) stays in the pasture.

Keep breathing, watching, and labeling. A thought is only a thought. An imaginary horse is just that, an imagination. Each thought does not require you to react. It doesn't make you do anything; it doesn't define who you are. Observe your thoughts as if they are just visiting horses passing in and out of the pasture. Let them have their brief moment. The important thing is to let them leave when they're ready to go and to label the next thought . . . and the next thought.

Continue this activity until you sense a real emotional distance from your thoughts. Wait until even the worrying thoughts are just moments in the pasture—no longer important, no longer impelling you to action. Practice this exercise at least once a day.

Dr. Harris reminds us that thoughts are just like stories: some are true, others fictional. In fact, since worry is always based on an unlikely maybe, it will almost always be fiction. Harris argues, "Thoughts are basically just stories: a bunch of words strung together to tell us something."[65] If you have a story that is bothersome, give the story a name, like the previous example of "Knucklehead." Now, when the story shows up, acknowledge it by name: "Oh, there it is, the old Knucklehead." Harris states, "You don't have to challenge it or push it away, nor do you have to give it much attention. Simply let it come and go as it pleases while you channel your energy into doing something you value."[66]

· · · · · · · · ·

Acceptance Activity 3: Expansion
Expansion is basically becoming friends with uncomfortable thoughts and feelings and includes four steps: observe, breathe, make space, and allow.

---

[65] *Harris, Russ. The Happiness Trap*
[66] *Harris, Russ. The Happiness Trap*

The following steps are summarized from the "The Happiness Trap."[67]

Step 1: Observe
With expansion, the observe step is different than the previous "observing" acceptance activity. With this activity, you will scan your body from head to toe, looking for sensations, focusing on those that may be uncomfortable. Perhaps there is an anxious feeling or a tightening in your chest or throat. Maybe there is pain in your back, neck, head, or behind your eyes. Once you pick a spot, bring your attention to the area, observing it with both kindness and curiosity. Dr. Harris would encourage you to:

> Notice where it starts and stops. If you had to draw an outline around this sensation, what shape would it have? Is it on the surface of the body, inside you, or both? How far inside does it go? Where is it most intense? Where is it the weakest? How is it different in the center than around the edges? Is there a pulse or vibration? Is it light or heavy? Moving or still? Warm or cool?[68]

Step 2: Breathe
The next step is to breathe—not just in and out, but actually send your breath into and around the sensation. Harris suggests the breaths be slow and deep, which will lower tension and bring a sense of calm, even an anchor. The uncomfortable feeling may not go away, but this should not be your goal.

Step 3: Create Space
As you breathe into and around the sensation, you will be creating some space around the feeling, giving it room to move and maybe even grow. Again, just notice the expansion with both kindness and curiosity.

Step 4: Allow
The final step is to allow the feeling to be there, even if you don't like it. Just let it be and don't fight any urges. If your mind starts making judgments, thank it and continue to observe, breathe, and create space. Of course, your habitual self will want to "cut and run" or return to any of your temporary relief remedies. Instead, sit, be still, and let it be. Harris says the goal is to "make peace with it, even if you don't like it or want it."[69]

---

[67] Harris, Russ. *The Happiness Trap*
[68] Harris, Russ. *The Happiness Trap*
[69] Harris, Russ. *The Happiness Trap*

Allow the feeling to persist for a few seconds or even minutes until you "completely give up the struggle with it." If this doesn't happen right away, that is okay. Remember, the goal is still acceptance.

. . . .

Acceptance Activity 4: Urge Surfing

Another very good acceptance activity is what Dr. Harris calls "urge surfing," which has five simple steps:[70]

1. Observe the urge (often anxiety), noticing where you feel it in your body.
2. Acknowledge it. Like, "I'm having the urge to . . . ."
3. Breathe into it and make room for it (don't try to get rid of it or suppress it).
4. Watch the urge as it rises, crests, and falls again. And, if the mind starts judging or telling you unhelpful stories, silently thank it. If the urge grows, just give it some space; soon it will crest and then fall again.
5. Check in with your values and ask yourself: "What action can I take right now—instead of trying to resist or control my urges—that will enhance my life? Then whatever the answer is, do it."[71]

A review of urge surfing will remind you of the basic principles of ACT (accept, choose, and take action).

I believe we can also look at acceptance from a gospel perspective. King Benjamin in the Book of Mormon taught:

> For the natural man is an enemy to God, and has been from the fall of Adam, and will be, forever and ever, unless he yields to the enticings of the Holy Spirit, and putteth off the natural man and becometh a saint through the atonement of Christ the Lord, and becometh as a child, submissive, meek, humble, patient, full of love, willing to submit to all things which the Lord seeth fit to inflict upon him, even as a child doth submit to his father.[72]

---

[70] *Harris, Russ. The Happiness Trap*
[71] *Harris, Russ. The Happiness Trap*
[72] *Mosiah 3:19*

As natural men and women, life will bring opposition and difficulties, and even God will inflict things upon us. If we accept and humbly "submit to all things," our capacity to "hold on" and "fear not" will be enabled by the "enticings of the Holy Spirit" and "the atonement of Christ the Lord."

> **Points to Ponder:** The opposite of avoidance is acceptance. All emotions have a lifespan. When we give up the fight with troublesome thoughts and feelings and just accept them, we will likely be surprised how quickly they flee.
>
> **Questions to Consider:** Am I ready to give up the fight with avoidance and practice the acceptance skills that will help me make peace with worry and anxiety? What are my feelings, concerns, and hopes as I review and understand the value of acceptance?

Notes, thoughts, resolutions . . .

Notes Continued . . .

"The past is inflexible, now is sacred;
we never really live in the future."
—Neal A. Maxwell

CHAPTER 8

BE PRESENT

- - - - - - -

ACCEPTANCE Exercise 3

Depression is often a result of our mourning the past—a history that did not live up to expectations. In contrast, the catalyst for worry is often fear of the future. It is centered in "what if" thinking. President Thomas S. Monson said, "Sometimes we let our thoughts of tomorrow take up too much of today. Daydreaming of the past and longing for the future may provide comfort but will not take the place of living in the present. This is the day of our opportunity, and we must grasp it."[73]

In this quote, President Monson nicely summarized the central tenet of mindfulness, which is being present or living in the moment. Jon Kabat-Zinn, Professor of Medicine and creator of the Stress Reduction Clinic at the University of Massachusetts Medical School, states, "Mindfulness means paying attention in a particular way; on purpose, **in the present moment**, and nonjudgmentally."[74]

Elder Neal A. Maxwell called this the "holy present." In a 1974 talk, he taught, "The past of each of us is now inflexible. We need to concentrate on what has been called 'the holy present,' for now is sacred; we never really live in the future. The holy gift of life always takes the form of now."[75]

Central to ACT is mindfulness or living in the moment. The first step is to accept life as it is, including our troublesome thoughts, feelings, and worries. The root of many of our challenges is how we habitually deal with worry and upsetting thoughts, the FEAR factor, as described by Hayes.

Have we ever lived in a more distracted age? Just look around you,

---

[73] *Ensign May 2003*
[74] *Kabat-Zinn, Jon. Mindfulness for Beginners*
[75] *Ensign November 1974*

even at church. So many don't even look up as they pass; they are either listening to something on some digital device or staring at some screen. I am just old enough to remember working at a desk before email and the Internet. Focus was so much easier then! I am just an email, text, or hyperlink away from my total attention being taken away from important tasks at hand. It affects my productivity, my capacity to communicate, and sometimes my happiness. To truly connect, we need to disconnect. The goal is to mindfully live in the moment. Living in the moment disengages our remembering and worrying mind and connects us with the "holy present." The result can be a tremendous gratitude for all God has given us. Again, the following activities will require practice, patience, and turning off any digital devices.

Connect Activity 1: Mindful Eating

I have a ten-year-old son, and watching him eat is a perfect example of not mindfully eating. In fact, I wonder if he even tastes his food. For him, dinner is just the thing between him and more play. This is true even when he eats candy, which is a puzzle. Taking the opposite approach is the key to mindful eating. As you eat, take time to really enjoy and savor each bite. Notice the aroma of each food item. Experience the texture in your mouth. Observe where on your tongue the taste buds are activated. Savor, experience, and enjoy every morsel and the entire eating experience.

. . . .

Connect Activity 2: Mindful Walking[76]

Take a break and go for a stroll. You can do this either indoors or out. It could be as simple as a walk down the hall or a jaunt around your building. You can walk fast, slow, or very slow; it doesn't really matter. The key is to focus on some aspect of your walking. It could be your gait, the feel of the earth under your feet, or even your breathing. I like to focus on the sights and sounds around me, particularly those I find in nature. The key is be present and simply notice the sensations in your feet, legs, hips, or arms. If your mind wanders, come back to whatever you are focusing on, whether it is sights, sounds, or sensations.

---

[76] *Adapted from "The Mindfulness and Acceptance Workbook for Anxiety;" Forsyth and Eifert 2008*

Connect Activity 3: Mindful Observance of Others

Are you a people watcher? This is one of my favorite pastimes in an airport. Find a place to sit and notice people as they pass by. Be careful not to be caught staring. Notice their facial features—do they seem happy or sad? Look for beauty in each person. It will be in their eyes, smile, or countenance. If they happen to look your way, respond with a smile and a kind gesture. Try looking at each one as a child of God and sense His love for them individually.

. . . .

Connect Activity 4: Notice 5 Things[77]

This is a simple exercise you can practice easily at any time or place.

1. Pause for a moment
2. Look around and notice five objects you can <u>see</u>
3. Listen carefully and notice five sounds you can <u>hear</u>
4. Notice five things you can <u>feel</u> against the surface of your body

You can include this activity with mindful walking, paying attention to what you see, hear, smell, and feel, always refocusing when your mind wanders.

. . . .

Connect Activity 5: Have a Positive Experience[78]

Instead of just pushing through with the busyness of life or trudging headlong to the next activity, take a few moments each day to intentionally have positive experiences. In his book, "Hardwiring Happiness," Dr. Richard Hansen reminds us that our natural [man] tendency is to be Teflon for the good and Velcro for the bad. To counter this, we should pause and HEAL, which stands for:

H: Have a positive experience

E: Enhance that experience

A: Absorb the experience

L: Link the positive with the negative

---

[77] *Adapted from "The Happiness Trap;" Harris 2008*
[78] *Adapted from "Hardwiring Happiness;" Hansen 2013*

For example, when I leave my office for my daily walk home I might recognize a storm is passing through. My natural tendency is to stick to this negatively, like Velcro. Rather, I can take a moment and pause, choosing to look at the storm in a positive light and have a better experience. I can notice the clean, refreshing smell of new rain and feel the crisp, cool air on my face. I can gaze at the beauty, shapes, and texture of the dark clouds rolling by. In short, I can enhance and absorb every positive aspect of the storm. There are dozens of times each day when you can choose to have a positive experience like the sunrise, a breeze on your cheek, the sun on your face, the smile from a loved one, or an embrace.

Sometimes we experience anxiety associated with past experiences. Especially in those situations, I need to choose to have a positive moment and link it to the negative. A positive and negative experience cannot occupy the same space, and overtime our brain will associate the event in a positive way. Dr. Hansen teaches, "neurons that fire together, wire together."[79] By practicing HEAL, sections of our brains will light up, creating new positive neural pathways. Overtime, this will result in more optimistic outlooks, all by connecting with the positive of now. Autumn, one of my students, shared how she learned to embrace the moment.

Autumn's Story

One of the ways Autumn was able to HEAL was by making a list of things she never wanted to "get used to." One of the top things on her list was that she never wants to get used to the mountains of Utah. She said, "I never want to forget they are there or how unreal they looked the first time I saw them. (I'm from Texas, which means the most elevation I grew up with was when we dug holes.) There are specific things that I run into throughout my day that are little reminders to look up and be mindful."

With practice, mindfulness can become a way of life. You can even bring mindfulness into your daily routine. For example, have you ever noticed just how pleasant washing your hands can be? Next time, feel the pleasant

---

[79] *Hanson, Rick. Hardwiring Happiness*

stream of warm water as it flows over your hands. Embrace and absorb every sensation of the water. Take a deep breath through your nose and smell the aroma of the soap. Likewise, you can do the same while showering, bathing, ironing a shirt, or brushing your teeth.

As you practice these exercises and become more skilled at living mindfully, you will gain a greater capacity to accept and embrace whatever life brings. In fact, just like Elder Joseph B. Wirthlin, you could adopt the phrase "come what may and love it."[80]

Points to Ponder: The key to mindfulness is living in the moment, or the "holy present." Living mindfully is a powerful antidote for both anxiety (fear of the future) and depression (mourning the past). Mindfulness can be a learned behavior and, with practice, become a way of life.

Questions to Consider: Am I ready to live in the moment? Am I committed to regular practice of these activities so I can make the most of each moment of each day? What blessings can I receive by learning to live in the "holy present?"

Notes, thoughts, resolutions . . .

---

[80] *Ensign May 2008*

Notes Continued. . .

Principle 2, Know:

We are children of God with divine worth and purpose; He gives us experiences for our good, and He will be with us forever and ever.

"As man now is, God once was; as God is now man may be."
—Lorenzo Snow

CHAPTER 9

KNOW

As we face worries and anxiety, the Lessons from Liberty Jail remind us that the most important **knows** are "all these things shall give [us] experience and be for our good" and "God will be with [us] forever and ever."[81] Sadly, challenges can become obsessive and elevated to how we define ourselves, sometimes sideswiping eternal perspectives. As we learned with acceptance – worries, anxieties, and fears are part of this mortal life. It is part of being a natural man or woman. Yet many can and do live very well with personality traits, worries, tendencies, and disabilities. How do they do this? The worry, disability, or tendency is just a part of them. It does not define who they are.

JUST A PART OF ME

I remember meeting a lovely young lady as a newly called campus bishop. During my first interview she said, "Hello, my name is Hannah, and I have depression." As we visited, I soon learned much more about her, and it was true; dealing with depression was part of who she was. Yet for her, it was such a big part of her life that it was how she had come to identify herself. She did not come in and say, "Hello Bishop, my name is Hannah, and I am an elementary education major from Oregon. My parents are Bob and Kathy, and I am a child of God."

In his conference talk titled "Finding Joy in Life," Elder Richard G. Scott provided a wonderful analogy on perspective and explained how we should remember that our trials are in reality just small parts of our lives.

---

[81] *Doctrine and Covenants 122:7,9*

He stated:

> A pebble held close to the eye appears to be a gigantic obstacle. Cast on the ground, it is seen in perspective. Likewise, [the] problems or trials in our lives need to be viewed in perspective... No matter how difficult something you or a loved one faces, it should not take over your life and be the center of all your interest. Challenges are growth experiences, temporary scenes to be played out on the background of a happy life. Don't become so absorbed in a single event that you can't think of anything else or care for yourself or for those who depend upon you.[82]

When I have become consumed with a particular concern, I sometimes fall into the "Hannah trap." I become obsessed with my top-of-mind worry. As people would say hello and "how are you?" my response could have been, "I'd be great if I wasn't such a worrier" (or a Downwinder, or a hypochondriac, or if I was sleeping better, etc.).

Are there challenges you deal with, perhaps a personality trait, a worry, a troublesome temptation, or a habit that has become how you identify yourself? When you look in the mirror and have a moment of self-reflection, what do you see? Take just a few minutes and write the top five things that come to mind:

1.

2.

3.

4.

5.

If there are character traits or personal struggles at the top of your list, they may have usurped roles that should matter most. When you look into a mirror and see your "real self," even as Heavenly Father sees you, your list should look like this:

---

[82] *Ensign May 1996*

1. A son or daughter of God, with divine worth
2. A disciple of Jesus Christ
3. A father, mother, sister or brother
4. A professional
5. Oh, and a worrier.

Yes, worry can be part of who you are, but it is just a part, not your whole life. In reality, this part of you is just a fraction of the whole, and if put into proper perspective a very small fraction—the little pebble cast to the ground. Often we are so hyper-focused on a particular worry that it climbs up the list and actually sidetracks us from focusing on the things that matter most, our important defining roles and values. Have you ever found yourself so distracted with a concern that you neglected someone or something you loved, perhaps because you were obsessed with a worry or wallowing in self-pity? Sadly, the obsession and pity will usually just compound the problem.

Hence, one of the beauties of ACT is that we accept our troublesome thoughts, acknowledge them, and put them in their proper perspective. Then we busy ourselves with things that truly matter: our values and causes. One of the benefits and the power of taking positive, value-based action is that it will also disrupt and change our negative thought patterns. In "The Greatest Salesman in the World," Og Mandino stated, "Weak is he who permits his thoughts to control his actions; strong is he who forces his actions to control his thoughts."[83] Could it be that acting on our values is the key to healing?

HEALING FROM AN ETERNAL PERSPECTIVE

When you accept your challenges and put them in proper perspective, there is a very good chance the particular worry or affliction will be temporary. The Lord, through the prophet Moroni, taught that our weakness can become our strength:

And if men come unto me I will show unto them their weakness. I give unto men weakness that they may be humble; and my grace is

---

[83] Mandino, Og. *The Greatest Salesman in the World*

sufficient for all men that humble themselves before me; for if they humble themselves before me, and have faith in me, then will I make weak things become strong unto them.[84]

In his talk "Do not Despair," President Ezra Taft Benson taught that we can experience complete healing:

"Salvation," said the Prophet Joseph Smith, "is nothing more nor less than to triumph over all our enemies and put them under our feet." We can rise above the enemies of despair, depression, discouragement, and despondency by remembering that God provides righteous alternatives.[85]

Yet we learn from the Apostle Paul that sometimes we may have the challenge of a more enduring trial:

And lest I should be exalted above measure through the abundance of the revelations, there was given to me a thorn in the flesh, the messenger of Satan to buffet me, lest I should be exalted above measure.

For this thing I besought the Lord thrice, that it might depart from me.

And he said unto me, my grace is sufficient for thee: for my strength is made perfect in weakness. Most gladly therefore will I rather glory in my infirmities, that the power of Christ may rest upon me.

Therefore I take pleasure in infirmities, in reproaches, in necessities, in persecutions, in distresses for Christ's sake: for when I am weak, then am I strong.[86]

Similarly, Elder Dallin H. Oaks stated:

Healing blessings come in many ways, each suited to our individual needs, as known to Him who loves us best. Sometimes a "healing" . . . lifts our burden. But sometimes we are "healed" by being given

---

[84] *Ether 12:27*
[85] *Ensign October 1986*
[86] *2 Corinthians 12:7–10*

strength or understanding or patience to bear the burdens placed upon us.[87]

When Paul stated, "I rather glory in my infirmities," and Elder Oaks said, "Sometimes we are . . . given strength, understanding, or patience," their advice sounds a lot like the core principle of ACT, which is acceptance. If we must accept our weakness, why not do so cheerfully?

Perhaps the greatest **know** is that through His Grace, we can be healed. I love how Jonathan Sandberg described the role of the Atonement in healing in his talk "Healing = Courage + Action + Grace":

> Grace is the power by which healing occurs. In every aspect of His mortal and post mortal ministry, Christ went about healing all manner of afflictions (see Matthew 9:18–25; 3 Nephi 17:9). His part is to be our atoning Savior, and our part is to be courageous enough to act. He then provides the grace and healing. However, sometimes we may not appreciate the manifestations of His grace because healing blessings do not always come in the form we ask. Sometimes His grace is made manifest by letting us sit and struggle with an issue. Again, our Heavenly Father and Savior are more interested in our growth and progression than in our comfort and convenience. Moments of struggle often bring the greatest growth.[88]

Sometimes we have to "sit and struggle" with worry and anxiety because the Savior is "interested in our growth" and healing will come if we are "courageous enough to act."

So, whether a weakness or trial is temporary, longer lasting, or an enduring event, in the end it doesn't really matter. When we understand the eternal nature of the Plan of Salvation, we can take great comfort in knowing that "all these things shall give [us] experience, and shall be for [our] good" and that "God shall be with [us] forever and ever."[89]

---

[87] Ensign *November 2006*

[88] *Sandberg, Brigham Young University Devotional 2014*

[89] *Doctrine and Covenants 122:9*

Points to Ponder: All of us have personality traits that are "just part of us" like worry. However, when we become obsessed with worry, anxiety, or fear, those concerns will take up an unhealthy portion of our life. Gaining the proper perspective that worry is "just a part of us" allows us to focus on our more divine and important roles and traits. The best way to put worry in its place is to discover our purpose and act on our values.

Questions to Consider: What are the things in my life, like worry, that have consumed too much of my time and energy? What actions can I take to put worry in its proper place as just a small part of who I am?

Notes, thoughts, resolutions . . .

Notes Continued. . .

"Rise to the stature of the divine within you."
—Gordon B. Hinckley

CHAPTER 10

CHOOSE VALUES

- - - - - - -

Practice 2: As we learn to "stand still" and know God, we will understand our divine nature and be inspired to discover our personal vision and <u>choose our values</u>.

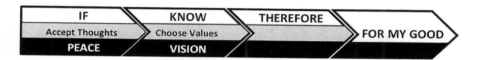

The second practice of ACT is to choose your values, which will be enhanced if you first discover your personal vision. In our busy lives, very few actually take time to consider, reflect on, and actually define either vision or values.

In the context of the lessons from Liberty Jail and ACT, the principle role of vision is to define who you want to become. The Lord sent the Prophet Joseph Smith and all of us a clarion call on what we should all aspire to, and that is to be both "called" and "chosen," blessed with the "rights of the priesthood" and the "powers of heaven."[90] After several warnings against pride, hiding our sins, selfish ambitions, and unhealthy authority, the Lord outlines the attributes that will help us become. They include:

- The virtue of the priesthood
- Persuasion
- Long suffering
- Gentleness
- Meekness
- Love
- Kindness

---

[90] *Doctrine and Covenants 121:34,36*

- Pure Knowledge
- Charity
- Virtue

A commitment to these values will result in promised blessings that will help us achieve our aspirations and eternal purposes. The Lord stated in D&C 121:45–46:

> Then shall thy confidence wax strong in the presence of God; and the doctrine of the priesthood shall distil upon thy soul as the dews from heaven. The Holy Ghost shall be thy constant companion, and thy scepter an unchanging scepter of righteousness and truth; and thy dominion shall be an everlasting dominion, and without compulsory means it shall flow unto thee forever and ever.[91]

While the lessons in the Liberty Jail revelations outline worthwhile characteristics and values, we should each spend some time identifying our own list of personal values, the "why's" or the reasons we do things. If we don't take the time to identify values, we may get out of alignment with both our internal and eternal purposes and become frustrated.

When we live by worry and fear, our personal vision and goals can be hijacked by distraction. Most have experienced this. Have you ever just felt "off" or that something is out of place? Usually, after some time for reflection, you will identify the problem. For example, one of my top values is my relationship with my wife. Yet, I can be unkind, impatient, selfish, or rule with "unrighteous dominion."[92] When I do so, my actions are not in alignment with this value, and I will suffer. My wife will tell you the root of my impatience and selfish inward focus are symptoms of chronic worry. Thankfully, the lessons from Liberty Jail and ACT provide principles, tools, and practices that will help you and I identify and live by our values, resulting in more productive living and a worthy diversion from unhealthy worry.

---

[91] *Doctrine and Covenants 121:45–46*
[92] *Doctrine and Covenants 121:39*

One way to look at both vision and values is to consider those things that you naturally want to do, things that are exciting, or that you love. Whenever we act, there is an underlying motivation. Some are very extrinsic, meaning we are being compelled. Others are more intrinsic, with the desire to act coming from within. Take just a moment and consider the bridge graphic below:

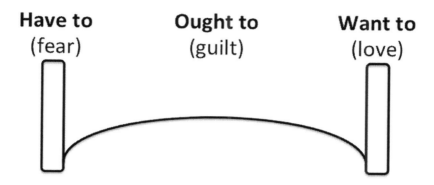

On the left side of the bridge, we are doing things that we have to do, and the motivation to act is usually because of fear. For example, "I have to do this or I will lose my job." As children, we did many things because we had a fear of punishment like doing our chores, practicing the piano, or not hitting a sibling. Sadly, this is how we as adults often parent or how our own parents motivated us to do certain things or stop doing others.

In the middle of the bridge are things we ought to do, and the motivation here is guilt or duty. We hate feeling guilty and will do all sorts of worthwhile activities mostly to avoid remorse. Checking things off our "ought to" lists motivates us. We do a lot of "middle of the bridge" things because guilt is uncomfortable. Examples could be church assignments, sending Christmas cards, and even taking cookies to the neighbors, especially if they extended a similar kind act.

On the right side of the bridge are those things we do because we want to, motivated by love. These are things we truly enjoy, those that bring us great satisfaction. We look forward to them with anticipation. Things we love to do are things we are converted to, and hopefully as we progress, our "want to's" include things like church callings, temple attendance, and serving others.

Former member of the Second Quorum of the Seventy, Elder Robert E. Sackley, challenged a group of missionaries to "cross the bridge." Happily, I was one of the elders learning this great lesson. On the chalkboard he drew a diagram of a bridge similar to the one used earlier. On one side of the bridge he wrote "man to man" and told us that if we were teaching just to reach a baptism goal or to make friends, we were on the wrong side. On the other side of the bridge he wrote "man to God" and challenged us to teach for the right reasons, to invite them to come unto Christ and be converted. As missionaries we crossed the bridge when we worked, served, and taught because we loved the people, loved His church, and loved the Savior. The more we crossed the bridge, the more we enjoyed the work, loved the people, and experienced real joy.

Doing things motivated by love is not limited to just spiritual endeavors. Steve Jobs, the founder of Apple Computers, said, "The only way to do great work is to love what you do. As with all matters of the heart you will know when you find it." Mala Grewal and Caroline Welty of the consulting firm The Talent Catalyst encourage people to discover their passion, even a profession that could rise to the level of a calling, something they want to do because they care. National statistics show that only 13 percent of Americans actually love their jobs. At 63 percent, the majority are mostly unhappy, and 24 percent actually hate their work.[93] The diagram below illustrates the differences between a job, a career, and a calling:[94]

Of Necessity   What Most Have   A Passion or Cause

---

[93] *Forbes October 10, 2013*
[94] *Adapted from the "The Talent Catalyst"*

The next time you ask someone "How's your job?" you might be surprised by his or her response. It could be an "ugh," "yuck," or "It's okay." If they say, "I love it," they have arrived at a calling or passion. They have "crossed the bridge" to a job aligned with their vision, who they want to become, and their core values.

In the next two chapters you will participate in practices designed to help you discover your passion and connect with your values. In preparation, let's set the stage by having you answer the following questions. Before you do so, take a few moments to be still using one of the mindfulness techniques you have already practiced.

What are the things you love to do? What are your "want to's"?

Do you have a cause you are passionate about?

What do your responses say about who you want to become?

> **Points to Ponder:** We find more joy and success when we do things because we want to, motivated by love. We find less happiness and fulfillment when and if our motivations are from fear or guilt.
>
> **Questions to Consider:** What are the things I love to do? Why do I love them? Am I doing them?

Notes, thoughts, resolutions . . .

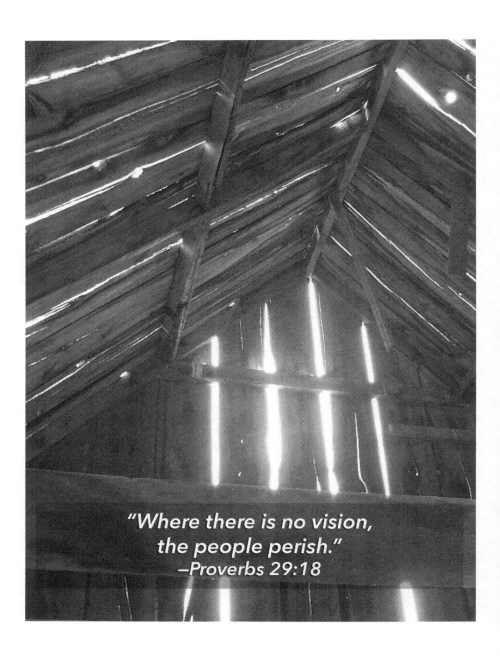

"Where there is no vision,
the people perish."
—Proverbs 29:18

CHAPTER 11

DISCOVER YOUR VISION

- - - - - - -

CHOOSE VALUES Exercise 1

Central to our personal vision is a sense of knowing who we are and what we can become. From an eternal perspective, the prophet Joseph Smith learned in Liberty Jail that God will "exalt [us] on high" and that we can "triumph over all [our] foes." This will especially be true if we can "endure it well."[95]

In recent times, the champion of personal vision and mission statements has been Stephen R. Covey. In his book, "The 7 Habits of Highly Effective People," he outlines the value of mission statements with habit number two, "begin with the end in mind." Thousands have attended Franklin Covey seminars across the world, which include extensive exercises on building mission statements. In these workshops, participants are first asked to list all of their current roles. Examples of roles could be husband, dad, daughter, church member, friend, and employee.

The second activity is to pick a significant person for each of those roles and then write down what they would hope that person would say about them if they were asked to speak at their funeral. Here is an example of what a husband would like to have his wife say: "He was a kind and loving father, totally devoted his family, our church, and his Heavenly Father."

The third step was to then take all of the summary statements and synthesize them into a mission statement. The participants would then be invited to take their new document, ponder and pray about it, rework it, and craft it into a statement that would both inspire and direct their lives.

In my university success course, I have used the mission statement writing tools of "The 7 Habits of Highly Effective People." Another

---

[95] *Doctrine and Covenants 121:8*

resource was David A. Christensen's "Inner Victory." Like Covey, he also focused on the importance of creating "your song" or mission statement. I have used both Covey's and Christensen's models and have read literally thousands of mission statements from students. Many of them are truly inspiring and have provided empowering personal direction. I have also researched the mission statements of several organizations and successful people. As a result, I have thought about, pondered, written, and rewritten my own personal mission statement many times. My early efforts resulted in fairly long versions loaded with values, hopes, goals, and aspirations. I remember Covey urging us to not only write our statement, but to commit it to memory. So I began to rethink, ponder, pray, and whittle my statement down to fewer words, which are:

As a disciple of Jesus Christ, I cheerfully help others find joy in Him.

I daily strive to:

- Know Him
- Trust Him
- Serve His children
- Become more like Him, and
- Thank Him

As I review and recite my mission statement, I am inclined to ponder and ask the question, "How am I doing?" As with all fallen and natural men, some days the answer is not so positive. However improvement is still something I strive for each day. While I do realize that I will not reach perfection in this life, my yearnings and efforts hopefully help me become a better person.

I also discovered two more resources on the value of purpose. The first was a 30-minute movie created by Dewitt Jones, a National Geographic photographer. He insightfully illustrated the power of vision and perspective. An example he gave was a project of taking pictures of dandelions in a high mountain meadow. When he arrived at the meadow, the light and setting was not just right, so he determined to postpone his photo-shoot until a later day. When he arrived the second time, he was a bit frustrated and chagrined because all of the dandelion flowers had transformed into puffballs. He now had a choice: he could be discouraged or change his perspective and celebrate his new circumstances. He elected to celebrate and took some amazing pictures of puffballs.

Through his efforts, he created a very brief and powerful vision statement: "Celebrate what's right with the world." Dewitt's invitation is for each of us to craft a simple statement that inspires, empowers, and in his case, gives both vision and perspective.

The second resource I have found useful is "How Will You Measure Your Life" by Harvard professor and former Latter-day Saint Area Authority Clayton Christensen. He describes the three parts of purpose as:

1. Likeness, or the person you want to become . . . and the kind of person God wants you to become.
2. Becoming committed to your likeness or aspirations so deeply that they guide what you prioritize on a daily basis.
3. Finding the right metric on how your life will be measured.

Clayton Christensen shares in "How Will You Measure Your Life" his likeness, or vision statement:

A man who is dedicated to helping improve the lives of other people

A kind, honest, forgiving, and selfless husband, father and friend

A man who just doesn't believe in God, but who believes God.[96]

I was struck by the simplicity and power of his three parts of personal vision. Two statements in his book really hit home. The first:

If you begin to feel that the likeness you have sketched out for yourself is not right—that this is not the person you want to become—then you must revisit your likeness. But if it becomes clear that it is the person you want to become, then you must devote your life to becoming that person.[97]

The second is regarding finding the right metric, which I assumed would

---

[96] *Christensen, Clayton. How will You Measure Your Life?*
[97] *Christensen, Clayton. How will You Measure Your Life?*

have been fairly complex with some sort of reporting system or scorecard so often used in corporate America. Instead, it was beautifully simple:

> I came to understand that while many of us might default to measuring our lives by summary statistics, such as number of people presided over, number of awards, or dollars accumulated in a bank . . . the only metrics that will truly matter to my life are the individuals whom I have been able to help, one by one, to become better people. When I have my interview with God, our conversation will focus on the individual's self-esteem I was able to strengthen, whose faith I was able to reinforce, on whose discomfort I was able to assuage -- a doer of good, regardless of what assignment I had. These are the metrics that matter in measuring my life.[98]

Here are just a few examples of personal mission statements. You will notice a variety of styles and lengths. In the end, your version should be uniquely you.

From Mother Teresa:

Life is an opportunity, benefit from it.

Life is beauty, admire it.

Life is a dream, realize it.

Life is a challenge, meet it.

Life is a duty, complete it.

Life is a game, play it.

Life is a promise, fulfill it.

Life is sorrow, overcome it.

Life is a song, sing it.

Life is a struggle, accept it.

Life is a tragedy, confront it.

Life is an adventure, dare it.

Life is luck, make it.

Life is too precious, do not destroy it.

Life is life, fight for it.

---

[98] *Christensen, Clayton. How will You Measure Your Life?*

I love this example from Elder Rolf Kerr, which was featured in "7 Habits:"

> Succeed at home first.
>
> Never compromise with honesty.
>
> Hear both sides before judging.
>
> Obtain the counsel of others.
>
> Defend those who are absent.
>
> Develop one new proficiency a year.
>
> Plan tomorrow's work today.
>
> Maintain a positive attitude.
>
> Keep a sense of humor.
>
> Be orderly in person and in work.
>
> Listen twice as much as you speak.
>
> Concentrate all abilities and efforts on the task at hand, not worrying about the next job or promotion.

Here is an example from one of my students Erinn Noble:

> I am a follower of my Savior Jesus Christ, and as such I will live my life as He lived His. I will be His comforter to those that need comfort. I will give all that I can to those who have little. I will not seek for recognition, but only seek to help others. When my time is ended here, I will know my Savior and He will know me.

FAMILY MISSIONS

Mission statements can provide direction and motivation for each of us individually. They can also have great power for families and organizations. Many families have taken the time to pray, ponder, discuss, and craft mission statements. Here is an example from Stephen Covey's "Personal Leadership Application Workbook:"

> <u>Our Family Mission</u>
> To love each other . . .
>
> To help each other . . .

To believe in each other . . .

To wisely use our time, talents, and resources to bless others . . .

To worship together . . .

Forever.

And my family's statement:

Our family is Christ-centered and temple–focused, and we will:

- Exercise faith
- Practice charity
- Seek the truth, and
- Obey the commandments

THE MISSION OF THE CHURCH

Largely because of Covey's work, many organizations created mission statements during the latter part of the 20th century. I don't know of a better example than that of the Church of Jesus Christ of Latter-day Saints. Since 1981, the Church has had a published mission. Over the years, the central purpose of this statement has remained the same, but it has been modified at least four times. In the April session of General Conference in 1981, President Spencer W. Kimball announced:

My brothers and sisters, as the Brethren of the First Presidency and the Twelve have meditated upon and prayed about the great latter-day work the Lord has given us to do, we are impressed that the mission of the Church is threefold:

- To proclaim the gospel of the Lord Jesus Christ to every nation, kindred, tongue, and people;
- To perfect the Saints by preparing them to receive the ordinances of the gospel and by instruction and discipline to gain exaltation;
- To redeem the dead by performing vicarious ordinances of the gospel for those who have lived on the earth.

All three are part of one work—to assist our Father in Heaven and His Son, Jesus Christ, in Their grand and glorious mission "to bring to

100

pass the immortality and eternal life of man." (Moses 1:39)[99]

Not only did this announcement proclaim the Church's mission, but the Lord's prophet affirmed the mission of the Father and the Son from Moses 1:39.

Sometime later, the official mission was modified to:

The Lord declared that it is His work and glory 'to bring to pass the immortality and eternal life of man' (Moses 1:39). He established His church to help with this great work. Accordingly, the Church's mission is to 'invite all to come unto Christ' (D&C 20:59) and 'be perfected in Him' (Moroni 10:32). This mission has three dimensions: (1) to proclaim the gospel of Jesus Christ to every nation, kindred, tongue and people; (2) perfect the saints by preparing them to receive ordinances of the gospel, and (3) redeem the dead by performing vicarious ordinances for them.

In this updated version, the focus on the Father and Son's role is moved to the beginning, and the phrase "invite all to come unto Christ and be perfected in Him" was added. Later, under the direction of President Thomas S. Monson, a fourth dimension was inserted, which states, "to care for the poor and the needy."

When Church handbooks were updated, the mission statement was again modified and shortened:

The Church of Jesus Christ of Latter-day Saints was organized by God to assist in His work to bring to pass the salvation and exaltation of His children. The Church invites all to "come unto Christ, and be perfected in Him" (Moroni 10:32; see also D&C 20:59). The invitation to come unto Christ pertains to all who have lived, or will ever live, on the earth.[100]

There are dozens of ways that you could approach building your mission or vision statement. For me, the key is to define who I want to become, and I believe becoming is an eternal process. Given I will always be becoming, a good exercise is to ponder how I would like to be described near the end of

---

[99] *Ensign May 1981*
[100] *"The Church of Jesus Christ of Latter-day Saints Handbook 2: Administering the Church 2.2"*

my time on earth and a consideration of the lessons from my life I would hold most valuable. The following activities will help you define who you want to become and provide a framework for your mission or vision statement.

Vision Activity 1 -- An Accurate Eulogy

Usually, when a person dies, someone will craft both an obituary and a life sketch or eulogy that are given at the funeral. Thankfully, these almost always highlight finer points and characteristics. Yet there will always be things left out. Imagine for a moment you were able, as a spirit, to participate in your funeral. Of course, you will be able to hear the speeches, life sketch, and eulogy. In this scenario, you will also be able to sit at the luncheon table with your dearest friends and family members. You will listen to each conversation. A little later, at the cemetery and your graveside, you can stand by and hear open and uncensored exchanges. In this setting, where your loved ones can speak with frankness, what would they say? Could it be, "Boy he had a temper!" or "she was such a worrier," or "It's too bad he never could get over his addiction to_____"? Rather, I am sure you would hope to hear, "She was so kind and such an example of Christian living," or "What integrity, courage, faithfulness, kindness, and patience she lived by."

In the space below, list the top three to five things you would like to have others say about you at your funeral. This activity will help as you craft your own personal mission statement.

Vision Activity 2 - Your Life's Lessons

Imagine it is near the end of your mortal life (perhaps your 90th birthday party), and you have an opportunity to gather immediate family members around you. Your audience includes your spouse, children, grandchildren, and great-grandchildren. Because of the circumstances, this may be the last time you have to visit with a large number of those you care for most. Picture one of your great-grandchildren asking you, "Grandpa or Grandma, what advice would you give us so we can be happy and successful in life?" What would be the top three to five things you would tell them?

· · · · · · · · ·

From these activities, what have you learned about your hopes, dreams, aspirations, and what you hope to become? Now, take a first stab at crafting your mission statement. At first, don't worry too much about the length, verbiage, or style. After you complete this first draft, take some time to read, review, ponder, and ask yourself, "Does this statement reflect who I am and who I want to be? Does it inspire me?"

You will want to revise this first draft, perhaps several times. Over time, it will begin to feel right and true to your ideal self. You will know you have arrived when, like Clayton Christensen taught, you are committed to the "likeness you want to become."[101]

I recommend creating a short statement, almost like a prelude or tagline to include with your personal mission. Two good examples are Dewitt Jones's "celebrate what's right with the world" and the Church's "invite all to come unto Christ and be perfected in Him."

---

[101] *Christensen, Clayton. How will You Measure Your Life?*

The first section of the worksheet provides space for a first draft of your personal mission. You will find extra copies of the entire worksheet at the back of the book or at https://lessonsfromlibertyjail.com.

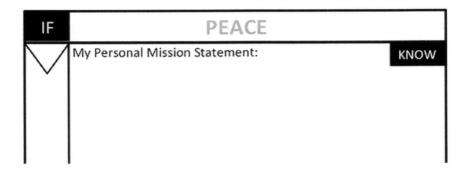

Points to Ponder: Successful people, families, and organizations have taken the time to define their vision or purpose. Most often, these are stated in mission statements. Mission statements provide direction and guideposts for almost all personal or group activities and inspire best efforts.

Questions to Consider: What is my personal vision, or the likeness I want to become? Have I created my own personal mission statement? If so, why does my mission statement inspire and motivate me to do better and be better?

Notes, thoughts, resolutions . . .

Notes continued . . .

"The two most important
days in your life are the day you are born
and the day you find out why."
-Mark Twain

CHAPTER 12

CONNECT WITH YOUR VALUES

- - - - - - -

CHOOSE VALUES Exercise 2

While vision gives us direction, values are the reasons why we do things. Values are the "whys" of life, the purpose behind our actions. The more powerful the why, the more the value will compel us to act. Viktor Frankl stated, "Those who have a 'why' to live, can bear with almost any 'how.'"[102]

THE TITLE OF LIBERTY

One of the best lessons on values can be found in the Book of Mormon. As a young reader, I was initially very interested in the war chapters in Alma. There was a lot of action! I often pondered why so much time and space was committed to endless battles. Other than the compelling story of the Stripling Warriors, it seemed to me a lot of wasted space. Fortunately, I was blessed to hear a lecture from David Christensen, then a religion professor and author of "Inner Victory." He taught that an important lesson in the war chapters is the story of Captain Moroni and the Title of Liberty, which is really a list of values the Nephites could rally behind. In Alma chapter forty-six, verse twelve, we read, "And it came to pass that he rent his coat; and he took a piece thereof, and wrote upon it—In memory of our God, our religion, and freedom, and our peace, our wives, and our children—and he fastened it upon the end of a pole."[103]

Captain Moroni and the Nephites had powerful values worth defending. In contrast, the apostate Nephites, Zoramites, and wicked Lamanites, under Amalickiah, were fighting for very different reasons. Their reasons were for greed and power, with a hope "to subject them [the Nephites] and bring them into bondage that they might establish a kingdom

---

[102] *Frankl, Victor. Man's Search for Meaning*
[103] *Alma 12:46*

unto themselves over all the land."[104]

In contrast, Moroni and his followers had more noble motives: "Nevertheless, the Nephites were inspired by a better cause, for they were not fighting for monarchy nor power but they were fighting for their homes and their liberties, their wives and their children, and their all, yea, for their rites of worship and their church."[105]

What are your "better causes?" The following activities will help you explore and identify those things that matter most—your values.

Value Identification Activity 1 -- Your Resource Allocation Process

In "How Will You Measure Your Life," Clayton Christensen urges his readers to look at how they expend their resources. He states:

> A strategy—whether in companies or in life—is created through hundreds of everyday decisions about how you spend your time, energy, and money. With every moment of your time, every decision about how you spend your energy and your money, you are making a statement about what really matters to you. You can talk all you want about having a clear purpose and strategy for your life, but ultimately this means nothing if you are not investing the resources you have in a way that is consistent with your strategy. In the end, a strategy is nothing but good intentions unless it's effectively implemented. How do you make sure that you're implementing the strategy you truly want to implement? Watch where your resources flow—the resource allocation process.[106]

Take just a few moments and consider the following:

1. When I have free time outside of the day-to-day demands of life, what do I do?

---

[104] *Alma 43:29*
[105] *Alma 43:45*
[106] *Christensen, Clayton. How will You Measure Your Life?*

2. What are the activities I most enjoy and are happy to spend my energy on?

3. When I have extra money, how do I spend it?

As you review your responses on how you spend your time, energy, and money, what personal values can you identify? Please list them in the space below:

Value Identification Activity 2 – A happy time/a sad time[107]
A Happy Day:

We are most happy when things are going well, when life is in balance and largely void of trials. Think for a moment and identify a time when you were the happiest. Be specific, like "I was most happy on December 3, 1985, when my first son was born."

Now, in the space below, record one of your happiest times:

Now ask yourself, why was this a most happy time?

As you consider your responses, what does this happy time say about what you value?

---

[107] *Adapted from "Inner Victory, Christensen, David 1995*

A Sad Day:

In contrast to your happiest moments, now reflect on a time that was especially difficult. Again, be specific. For example, "A time I was most sad was in the summer of 2014 when I learned that my good friend and business partner was leaving our company."

Again ask yourself, why was this a most difficult and sad time?

What does this most sad time say about your values?

. . . .

Value Identification Activity 3 -- What would you risk your life for?[108]

Imagine you just happened upon a tragic scene like a home on fire, a car partially submerged in a river and filling up, or a collapsed building that is very unstable. Perhaps this is your home in flames.

What would you be willing to put yourself in danger to rescue or retrieve?

What do your responses say about what you value enough to risk your life?

. . . .

Value Identification Activity 4 --From Vision to Value

Another activity to help you define your values is to review your vision or mission statement and pull out any values. For example, let's consider Clayton Christensen's vision statement and then identify his values:

A man who is dedicated to helping improve the lives of other people

A kind, honest, forgiving, and selfless husband, father and friend

A man who just doesn't believe in God, but who believes God

---

[108] *Adapted from "Inner Victory, Christensen, David 1995*

Some of his values could be:

- Dedication
- Service
- Kindness
- Honesty
- Dedication as a spouse
- Love for his children
- Care for his friends
- Faithfulness
- Trust in Heavenly Father

As you review the mission or vision statement you have created, what does it say about your values? Record your thoughts in the space below:

. . . .

As you have completed these activities, you should notice many of the same values in each activity. From these activities, make a list of your top five to ten values and record them according to rank with your most important value as number one. Identifying these values will help as you practice the "choose" part of ACT.

1.

2.

3.

4.

5.

6.

7.

8.

9.

10.

MEN ARE THAT THEY MIGHT HAVE JOY

We know living by values brings happiness and peace, but does it matter how we prioritize those thing that matter most? Can we learn from the Savior's teachings about what things should come first? In Matthew chapter twenty-two, we read of the Savior's response to the Pharisee who asked: "Which is the great commandment in the law?"[109] Jesus responded, "Thou shalt love the Lord thy God with all thy heart, and with all thy soul, and with all thy mind. This is the first and great commandment. And the second is like unto it, Thou shalt love thy neighbor as thyself. On these two commandments hang all the law and the prophets."[110]

In 2 Nephi chapter two verse 25, we learn that in this life "we might have joy."[111] One way to remember the path to joy is to turn it into the acronym JOY:

J - Jesus first

O - Others second

Y - Yourself third

While this is not the literal interpretation of this scripture, it is a good reminder that true happiness, joy, and salvation comes through believing in, becoming converted to, and following the two great commandments.

In my studies, I have come across three very good books illustrating the importance of putting deity and others before ourselves. The first is titled "I am Third." It was written by pro-football Hall-of-Famer Gale Sayers and was the inspiration for the movie "Brian's Song." In this memoir, Sayers recounts the struggle of seeing his best friend and teammate battle and eventually lose his battle with lung cancer. Sayers himself endured tragic knee injuries that cut short his career. He lived his life by this creed: "The Lord is first, my friends are second, and I am third."[112]

---

[109] *Matthew 22:36*
[110] *Matthew 22:37–40*
[111] *2 Nephi 5:22*
[112] *Sayers, Gale. I Am Third*

The second is "A Season of Life" by Jeffrey Marx. In this Pulitzer Prize winning book, Marx tells the story of Joe Ehrmann, a former pro-football all-star. After witnessing the early death of his younger brother, he turned his life over to God and served others. As a minister, he created the program "Men Built for Others," and as volunteer football coach emphasized "relationships and having a cause bigger than yourself."[113]

Finally, the Latter-day Saint author Ester Rasband, in "Confronting the Myth of Self Esteem," illustrates that the path to peace is not a focus on self, but rather on service to our Heavenly Father, His kingdom, and others. She emphasized the Christian paradox: to find ourselves, we must first lose ourselves in the service of others.[114]

President Spencer W. Kimball taught this paradox beautifully when he said:

> Only when you lift a burden, God will lift your burden. Divine paradox this. The man who staggers and falls because his burden is too great can lighten that burden by taking on the weight of another's burden. You get by giving, but your part of giving must be given first.[115]

Consider for a moment the JOY principle and look again at the values you just listed. Place a J next to the values if they are closely associated with Heavenly Father, His Son, or His Church. Now, place an O next to the values related to others, including your family and friends. Finally, place a Y next to those related to you. Since peace and joy come from loving God and serving others, perhaps you could consider re-ranking your values using the JOY model.

Please note, all aspects of JOY are important, including those of a very personal nature. It would be very difficult to serve God and others when you are not taking care of yourself.

Combining Purpose and Values

Now that you have discovered and recorded your vision and identified your top values, I recommend you combine them into one statement. Here is an

---

[113] *Marx, Jeffrey. Season of Life*
[114] *Rasband, Ester. Confronting the Myth of Self-Esteem*
[115] *Kimball, Spencer W. The Teachings of Spencer W. Kimball*

example:

As a disciple of Jesus Christ, I cheerfully help others find JOY in Him.

I daily strive to:

- Know Him
- Trust Him
- Serve His children
- Become more like Him, and
- Thank Him

These things matter most:

1. My relationship with my Heavenly Father and His Son (J)
2. My membership in His Church (J)
3. Having the companionship of the Holy Ghost (J)
4. My relationship with my wife (O)
5. Being a good father to my children (O)
6. Serving others (O)
7. Having a healthy body (Y)
8. Being the master of my emotions (Y)
9. Doing an outstanding job in my profession (Y)

· · · · · · · · ·

The next activity, adapted from Forsyth and Eifert in "The Mindfulness & Acceptance Workbook for Anxiety," will help you determine where you are in relationship to each of your values.

Valued Direction Activity[116]

From chapters 11 and 12, you now should have a personal mission statement and a list of your most important values. This exercise will help you make a personal assessment of how you are doing with each value. Socrates said, "The unexamined life is not worth living." This activity is a chance to examine how you are doing—to see what exactly you are sowing and reaping in the harvest of life. This honest assessment may be a bit uncomfortable, but with your capacity to make space, the quiet promptings

---

[116] *Adapted from "The Mindfulness and Acceptance Workbook for Anxiety;" Forsyth and Eifert 2008*

from the Holy Ghost and Light of Christ will help you discern the changes you need to make.

The first step is to pick a value to review. You will then rate the importance of the value and make an honest assessment of your personal satisfaction with that value. Here is an example:

Value: My relationship with my wife

IMPORTANCE: 0---------1---------2---------3---------4-------X

SATISFACTION: 0---------1---------2-----X--3---------4-------5

On this scale, I first put a large X where this value ranks in importance, with five representing an extremely important value. In this example, my relationship with my wife is a five.

The second step is to place an X on the scale giving an honest ranking of your current level of satisfaction regarding this value. Hopefully, the X on importance and the X for satisfaction are the same and at the high end of both scales. Realistically, however, you and I may have discrepancies, and it will be those disparities that contribute to suffering.

The third step is to ask some very important questions. In your honest answers, make sure you are examining your life and actions, not others.

1. Is there a discrepancy?
    Yes

2. If yes, why?
    I have been too busy at work and with my personal distractions. I have not spent enough one-on-one time with my wife.

3. What are the barriers?
    I am spending too much time following my favorite sports teams online. Honestly, I am more inclined to spend time interacting and playing with my kids. I need to avoid the temptation to stay late at work.

4.   What are the one or two things I can do to increase my satisfaction on this value?

Plan a date with my wife each week and make it a priority.
Unplug and spend time each day just visiting with her.

Now it is your turn. The worksheet includes a section for you to list and review each value. Take your time, be honest, and listen for promptings. The JOY acronym is provided so you can identify where the value fits by circling the appropriate letter. You will want to use the extra copies of the worksheet, provided at the back of the book (or online at https://www.lessonsfromlibertyjail.com), to accommodate all of your values.

VISION

J O Y

One of my important values is:

Importance: ────────────────────────
0 — Not important   3 — Moderately Important   5 — Very Important

Satisfaction: ────────────────────────
0 — Not Satisfied   3 — Moderately Satisfied   5 — Very Satisfied

Is there a discrepancy? If so, why?

Are there things I should stop or start doing?

What are the one or two things you can do to increase your satisfaction on this value?

If you are like me, this activity will result in two things: first, guilt, and second, a list of things to do or change. Both may be ouches. Thankfully, guilt can be a great motivator. Elder David A. Bednar said, "Guilt is to our spirit what pain is to our body—a warning of danger and a protection from additional damage."[117]

So, what does all this effort in defining a mission statement and values have to do with worry and anxiety? Nearly all actions are preceded by thoughts. Thoughts are followed by actions. Worries are thoughts and often prompt negative or self-defeating behaviors. Because negative thoughts usually cause emotional pain like anxiety, we go to all efforts to banish the pain. These efforts are usually related to aversion or attachment and, by nature, create new negative triggers. We are then trapped in the worry, anxiety, and negative action loop (see diagram below):

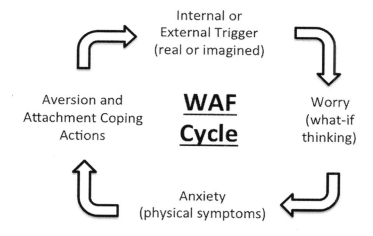

The ACT model disrupts this negative cycle by accepting worry and anxiety, reconnecting with values, and then taking proactive action based on personal vision and values. As the model below illustrates, taking positive value based action can disrupt the return of real or imagined triggers, thus breaking the cycle.

---

[117] *Ensign April 2013*

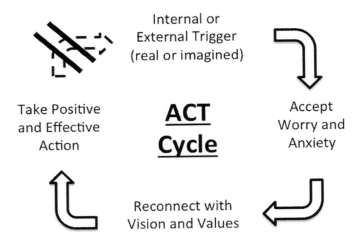

Internal or External Trigger (real or imagined)

Take Positive and Effective Action

ACT Cycle

Accept Worry and Anxiety

Reconnect with Vision and Values

Will this eliminate all adversity and the associated worry and anxiety? No. But when we accept worry and then positively act on our values, the cycle can be disrupted. A focus on values and positive action can relegate worry to its proper perspective—just a small part of life.

Points to Ponder: Values are why we do things, our beliefs in action. We live progressively when we focus on those things that matter most. We will be blessed if we follow the teachings of the Savior and place our values in priority order using the JOY (Jesus first, others second, yourself third) principle.

Questions to Consider: What are my values? Have I prioritized my values using the JOY model? How can I be more committed to living by my values, taking care of those things that matter most?

Notes, thoughts, resolutions . . .

Principle 3, Therefore:

To live up to our full potential and receive all of our foreordained blessings, we must take action.

"You can't plow a field simply by turning it over in your mind."
-Gordon B. Hinckley

CHAPTER 13

THEREFORE

As stated earlier, in the Liberty Jail revelations the Lord gives the Prophet Joseph Smith several **therefores**, which include the call to hold on and fear not. He also admonishes the prophet to be cheerful, act, be still, have faith, and have the patience to wait on the Lord until His salvation and hand were revealed.[118]

These could be the customary **therefores** for each of us as we face personal trials. However, in my mind the word **therefore** also represents the transition from values to action. Before we explore the final step in our model, take action; let's explore three very powerful **therefores** that could be added to the Liberty Jail standards.

THEREFORE STOP

The first is **therefore stop**. Because all of us have the Light of Christ, and many reading this book also have the Gift of the Holy Ghost, the things we should stop should be easy to identify. Are there things in your life that are driving away the spirit? Things like viewing pornography, substance abuse, or being dishonest? Others may be more minor offenses like murmuring, jealousy, or gossiping. A very important subject when considering the things we should stop is to determine if something has become an addiction. If so, seek help now! The Church has wonderful resources and has partnered with the Addiction Recovery Program.

Therefore stop can also apply to activities or habits that negatively impact our capacity to reach our goals. This could be things like procrastination, grumbling, being overly distracted by media, or self-

---

[118] *Doctrine and Covenants 123:17*

defeating behaviors.

Some of the items will be associated with habits of worry and efforts to avoid anxiety. The ACT practices can be very effective in breaking these habits and replacing them with more positive actions and thought patterns. President Spencer W. Kimball, in "The Miracle of Forgiveness," states:

> The devil knows where to tempt, where to put in his telling blows. He finds the vulnerable spot. Where one was weak before, he will be most easily tempted again . . . In abandoning sin one cannot merely wish for better conditions. He must make them . . . He must eliminate anything which would stir the old memories . . . Does this mean that the man who has quit smoking or drinking or had sex pollutions finds life empty for a time? The things which engaged him and caught his fancy and occupied his thoughts are gone, and better substitutions have not yet filled the void. This is Satan's opportunity. The man makes a start but may find the loss of yesterday's habits so great that he is enticed to return to his evil ways, and his lot thus becomes infinitely worsened. Many who have discontinued bad habits have found that substitution is part of the answer, and have conquered a bad habit by replacing it with a good or harmless one.[119]

In short, change and repentance require not only eliminating the negatives in our lives but also replacing them with positive attitudes and value-based actions.

When it comes to identifying habits or actions to eliminate, we should remember President Dieter F. Uchtdorf's two-word sermon, "stop it!"[120] What are your **therefore stops**? The things you know in your heart you should stop doing? Please record them in the space below:

---

[119] *Kimball, Spencer W. The Miracle of Forgiveness*
[120] *Ensign May 2012*

THEREFORE START

The second is **therefore start.** What are the things you know in your heart and mind you should start doing? What are the activities, plans, or assignments where procrastination or fear have gotten the best of you? I attended a conference in Salt Lake City, and one of the speakers challenged everyone in the audience to think of the one thing each of us would like to do but had not started. He then challenged us to take action. A personal example is this book. For years I have been mulling around the idea of writing a book related to personal productivity. I even added it to my bucket list. What did it take to get off of square one? Just starting. First an outline, then a sentence followed by a paragraph, and soon the momentum arrived and inspiration followed.

Interestingly, modern research is validating the value of many of the tried and true practices that are a part of the restored gospel and things each of us should start. For example, how often have we heard church leaders extol the virtues of gratitude, keeping a journal, meditation, exercise, and service? Recently, Shawn Achor, a Harvard professor, and author, has received national attention. In his Ted talk and book, "The Happiness Advantage," Achor argues against the human tendency to seek success to become happy. Instead, he states just the opposite is true—positivity will lead to more productivity, resulting in more happiness.[121] Achor's research indicates five simple daily activities that can have a major impact on our productivity and happiness, all scientifically proven to help with worry, anxiety, and depression:

1. **Three gratitudes** is the activity of recording three new things you are grateful for each day. Achor suggests if you will do this consistently over just a few weeks, you will have a more positive outlook on life. President Thomas S. Monson, from a more spiritual perspective, taught, "We can lift ourselves, and others as well, when we refuse to remain in the realm of negative thought and cultivate within our hearts an attitude of gratitude. If ingratitude be numbered among the serious sins, then gratitude takes its place among the noblest of virtues."[122]

---

[121] *Achor, Shawn. The Happiness Advantage*
[122] *Ensign May 1992*

2. **Journaling** about things that you are thankful for has been scientifically proven to be of great value to individuals, as shown in Achor's book. While his sources are secular, the valuable message is very similar to the lesson President Henry B. Eyring shared in his hallmark talk "Oh Remember, Remember":

> Tonight, and tomorrow night, you might pray and ponder, asking the questions: Did God send a message that was just for me? Did I see His hand in my life or the lives of my children? I will do that. And then I will find a way to preserve that memory for the day that I, and those that I love, will need to remember how much God loves us and how much we need Him. I testify that He loves us and blesses us, more than most of us have yet recognized. I know that is true, and it brings me joy to remember Him.[123]

3. **Exercise** is a great way to help overcome the struggle that comes with worry, anxiety, and depression. A report from the Center of Disease Control states that physical activity can help:

- Control weight
- Reduce risk of cardiovascular disease
- Reduce risk for type 2 diabetes
- Reduce risk of some cancers
- Strengthen bones and muscles
- Improve mental health and mood
- Improve ability to do daily activities
- Increase your chances of living longer

4. **Meditation**, like exercise, is becoming a must-do for those dealing with stress, anxiety, and depression. Countless studies have shown the benefits of regular meditation. One article reviewed how this activity could temper the effects of aging; calm down a wandering, worry-filled mind; help with social anxiety; improve concentration; and alleviate depression.[124] A Harvard study conducted in 2011 showed that meditation could actually change the structure of the

[123] *Ensign November 2007*
[124] *Forbes.com, February 9, 2015*

brain, increasing the sections responsible for learning and memory, while shrinking those for anxiety and fear. After just eight weeks of mindfulness-based stress reduction, those in the study reported decreased levels of stress.[125]

In his May 2014 CES devotional, Elder Russell M. Nelson, stated:

> Everyone needs time to meditate and contemplate. Even the Savior of the world, during His mortal ministry, found time to do so: "And when He had sent the multitudes away, He went up into a mountain apart to pray: and when the evening was come, He was there alone."
>
> We all need time to ask ourselves questions or to have a regular personal interview with ourselves. We are often so busy and the world is so loud that it is difficult to hear the heavenly words 'be still, and know that I am God.'

5. **Random acts of kindness** have been proven to create a boost in happiness in those who consciously serve others. These acts could be as simple as sending someone a message by email or by phone expressing gratitude and love. When acts of service are aligned with personal goals and values, they will be particularly rewarding and effective. President Thomas S. Monson taught, "Happiness comes through serving our Heavenly Father and serving our fellowmen."[126] More recently, President Dieter F. Uchtdorf said, "When we reach out to bless the lives of others, our lives are blessed as well. Service and sacrifice open the windows of heaven, allowing choice blessings to descend upon us. Surely our beloved Heavenly Father smiles upon those who care for the least of His children."[127]

If you were to add to these steps scripture study and personal prayer, your daily routine would be aligned with the teachings of the Church. Additionally, ACT is based on mindfulness, which includes the activity of meditation. I believe meditation can be enhanced if it includes a focus on

---

[125] *Harvard Gazette, January 21, 2011*
[126] *Ensign May 1988*
[127] *Ensign November 2008*

the Savior.

CHRIST-CENTERED MEDITATION

Both ancient eastern traditions and modern science have proven the value of meditation. Modern revelation and the scriptures teach the value of reflection, pondering, and taking time to be still, mostly because doing so increases our capacity to listen to promptings and improves our ability to act. In Dr. Gary Purse's webcast, "Abiding in the Stillands: Christ Centered Meditation,"[128] he taught the usefulness of the Bridle Meditations. We are reminded in Alma 38:12 to "bridle all our passions, that we may be filled with love."

The first activity is to **be still**, which is similar to the breath meditations we have already reviewed and hopefully you are practicing. Again, this practice helps us to create some space, to "mind the gap," increasing our capacity to tap into the Light of Christ and the Holy Ghost. This is where agency allows us to be blessed by the enabling power of the Atonement. Dr. Purse's instructions are very simple:

> Take some time every day to be still—close to the same time—to sit in silence in a quiet place and just breathe gently for 5–30 minutes. Sit with good posture (but not too stiff) in a comfortable chair, with hands and arms and legs unfolded, with feet on the floor. Keep your eyes open or closed, depending on the context and what is most relaxing for you.

> Don't try to get rid of your thoughts, or "clear your mind," but rather just watch your thoughts/moods/feelings like a movie. Let them come or go without clinging judgment or attachment. Our thoughts are like horses, small ponies, sometimes rodeo horses, or, as big as draft horses. Don't saddle the horses and ride them off. Don't feed them or try to rope them, just let them come and go. You can even label them as good, bad, or neutral, just don't cling to them.

> Focus on your breath—long, slow, deep, gentle. This is the first exercise in preparation for deepening your mindfulness. Try to avoid getting lost in your thoughts. When you start to drift from the present

---

[128] *Purse, Gary. BYU-Idaho Alumni Webcast*

moment, come back to your breath. Stay there for as long as you can.

The second bridle meditation is **to remember**, which aligns with vision and values, focusing on those things for which we are grateful. In almost all cases, those things we value and what we are thankful for will be the same. Dr. Purse's instructions for this practice are:

> A remembrance meditation directs your concentration to all blessings, tender mercies, kindness of others, and simple joys in your life. It is like an extended prayer of gratitude to Heavenly Father. Start out with "Heavenly Father I am grateful for," then just let the thoughts of gratitude flow naturally. They will often be given to you through the Spirit. Inventory your lifetime of blessings anyway you want to divide them up -- this hour, this week, this month, a certain time period, a location, etc. You could also just focus on people who have been deliberately kind to you. Be sure to direct your gratitude first on the Lord, and then to the people involved—but don't lose focus on your breath.

The third activity is **to serve** and correlates well with taking action. The instructions for this activity are:

> This is a meditation wherein you ponder or meditate on the welfare of others. This is like an extended prayer on behalf of others without losing track of your breath. Just start out the meditation thinking, "Dear Heavenly Father, please bless _____," and then let people come and go in your mind. Start first with the "beloved" people in your life. Then think of the "neutrals." These are people you may not know, or, just nameless people who have served or helped you in some way—people in society that make things better for all of us. Finally, turn your meditative attention to what I call the "angsters," those people who invite angst from us. Send love and best wishes to them—with the help of the Atonement—and ask Heavenly Father to bless them. The miracle is that if we do this, the Lord will sometimes give us the desire and words to offer in our minds during the meditation.

The final bridle meditation is to **let go**, which is very synonymous with acceptance, bringing us back to the foundation for ACT. This practice is to:

> Just rest in your awareness. Your only "work" is to not cling to your

concentrations. When you start to feel attachments, go back to your breath. Rest, observe, and let go. Don't cling to anything or try to figure out anything -- just rest in bare attention. Remember, you have dedicated this meditation to the Savior making space for enlightenment -- that may come in the moment or later, depending on His will.

Now that you have reviewed these wonderful meditation activities and listened for promptings, what are a few of things you would like to start doing? Record them below:

THEREFORE ACCEPT

The final is **therefore accept**. Some of our angst may be a result of our incapacity to accept the things we cannot change. Once again, this concept is taught so plainly in the Serenity Prayer, "God, grant me the serenity to **accept** the things I cannot change, the courage to change the things I can, and the wisdom to know the difference" (emphasis added).

Take a moment and consider a current concern or worry that you have. Does it involve another person and their agency? Perhaps, through your love and example, you may exert some positive influence for good. Unfortunately, it is often the case that your worry will have no realistic hope of making a difference, so in the end it will only result in needless suffering.

In his book "The Worry Solution," Dr. Martin Rossman, M.D., urges his readers to place the things they worry about into three categories: (1) things they can possibly change, (2) those they are not sure about, and (3) concerns they cannot change. He then invites the reader to assign a number to each worry (based on a 0–10 scale) rating the amount of anxiety or stress caused by the worry.[129].

---

[129] *Rossman, Martin. The Worry Solution*

Can Possibly Change	Not Sure	Cannot Change

A valuable activity would be to make a list of all of your current worries and place them in the table based on your best judgment on whether the concern is something you can realistically resolve. For example, my wife's 90-year-old father recently moved to our town to be close to two of his daughters. He enjoyed relatively good health until he was diagnosed with colon cancer and mild heart problems. Both his long-term and short-term care became the responsibility of his family and, in particular, my wife and her sister. His health challenges, family dynamics, and financial concerns were just part of a whole new list of concerns and worries. My wife's "worry list" could have looked something like this:

1. Father's overall health
2. Father's overall care
3. Medical expenses
4. Balancing support from family members
5. His overall mental well-being
6. The possibility of the cancer spreading
7. Relationships with other caregivers
8. Differing opinions on options

The next step is to place each worry in the table according to your best guess on whether or not you can resolve the issue. Here is an example on how my wife could have assigned and evaluated her concerns:

Can Possibly Change	Not Sure	Cannot Change
Relationships with other caregivers (8)	Father's overall health (8)	Will the cancer spread? (5)
Father's Overall Care (8)	His overall mental well-being (8)	Differing opinions on options (4)
Medical expenses (7)		
Balancing support from family members (5)		

Using this scenario, if and when my wife finds herself worrying about cancer growth in her father, this exercise could remind her she cannot really change the situation and it would be best to just let it go. Other worries, especially those in the "can possibly change" column and those that are causing much anxiety, should be dealt with by taking effective action. In this example, her relationship with the other caregivers is a big worry and one she could act on. For worries in the "not sure" category, she could do a little more research or seek additional support. With more information the worry might be moved to either the "can possibly change," or "cannot change" and then dealt with accordingly. Is there a particular worry that you have or are dealing with that a serious contemplation would lead you to the conclusion that it is something you cannot change? If so, ACT provides a healthy pattern – just accept it, re-connect with a value you can impact, and then take action.

As you have made a list of stops, starts, and things to accept, you could be thinking there are a lot of "to do's" and "not to do's," and you are likely feeling a bit overwhelmed—maybe a lot. Perhaps you will be inclined, even motivated, to start making changes, perhaps setting some goals. Just hold onto those thoughts for now; we will tackle effective change and goal setting in future chapters.

Points to Ponder: Healing and productive living comes as we take action. We should start doing things we need to be doing. We may need to stop doing things that are counterproductive or not in alignment with our vision and values. We will also be blessed if we can accept and act on those things we can change and avoid those we cannot.

Questions to Consider: Do I regularly take action? What can I start doing to be more anxiously engaged in good causes? What are the things of no worth I need to sop? Am I an accepting person? How can I stop wasting time and emotional energy on those things I likely cannot change?

Notes, thoughts, resolutions . .

"My dreams are worthless, my plans are dust, my goals are impossible . . . unless they are followed by action."
-Og Mandino

CHAPTER 14

TAKE ACTION

- - - - - - -

Practice 3: <u>Taking action</u> is more effective when we have a clear understanding of our goals and the steps to achieve them.

IF	KNOW	THEREFORE	
Accept Thoughts	Choose Values	Take Action	FOR MY GOOD
PEACE	VISION	AGENCY	BECOME

In "Taking the Leap," Pema Chodron reminds us that healing comes when we "sit and stay." When we take time to be still and meditate, we will naturally know what we should do. As we choose to stay with our uncomfortable emotions and "don't cut and run," we realize most of our dragons are imaginary, and many tigers are made of paper. The fourth step of ACT is to act on our values. In my opinion, "sit and stay" is a good start, but more effective healing happens when we get up out of our chairs and are "anxiously engaged in good causes." C.S. Lewis stated, "The more often he feels without acting, the less he will be able ever to act, and, in the long run, the less he will be able to feel."

The Lord revealed in D&C 58:26–27:

> For behold, it is not meet that I should command in all things; for he that is compelled in all things, the same is a slothful and not a wise servant; wherefore he receiveth no reward.
>
> Verily I say, men should be anxiously engaged in a good cause, and do many things of their own free will, and bring to pass much righteousness;
>
> For the power is in them, wherein they are agents unto themselves. And inasmuch as men do good they shall in nowise lose their reward.

What are your good causes? Once again, you should look at your mission statement, the listing of your values, and consider the JOY factor. The most

133

compelling causes, and those with promised blessings, are actions that can serve Heavenly Father, His church, and His children.

Recent findings in neuroscience by university professor Dr. Jason Hunt have shown the same centers of the brain that are associated with willpower are those linked to selfless service.[130] When we selflessly serve others, neuro-pathways are strengthened in just the right part of our brain that will increase our capacity to resist temptations, change habits, and overcome addictions. This is evidence that "all flesh is in His hands," including the grey matter between our ears. When we lose ourselves in the service of others,[131] we not only find ourselves, but our capacity to overcome weakness is enhanced.[132]

My favorite treatise on the value of taking action is found in Og Mandino's "The Greatest Salesman in the World." Og states:

My procrastination which has held me back was born of fear and now I recognize this secret mined from the depths of courageous hearts. Now I know that to conquer fear I must always act without hesitation and the flutters in my heart will vanish. Now I know that action reduces the lion of terror to an ant of equanimity. I will act now.

Henceforth, I will remember the lesson of the firefly who gives off its light only when it is on the wing, only when it is in action. I will become a firefly and even in the day my glow will be seen in spite of the sun. Let others be as butterflies who preen their wings yet depend on the charity of a flower for life. I will be as the firefly and my light will brighten the world.[133]

The number one enemy of taking action is procrastination. Often, the root of procrastination is fear. Ironically, the antidote for both is to take action.

Elder Bednar, in his talk, "Seek Learning by Faith," extolled the value of acting:

---

[130] Hunt, Jason. BYU-Idaho Alumni Webcast
[131] Matthew 16:25
[132] Ether 12:27
[133] Mandino, Og. The Greatest Salesman in the World

In the grand division of all of God's creations, there are things to act and things to be acted upon (see 2 Nephi 2:13–14). As sons and daughters of our Heavenly Father, we have been blessed with the gift of agency—the capacity and power of independent action. Endowed with agency, we are agents, and we **primarily are to act** and not only to be acted upon—especially as we seek to obtain and apply spiritual knowledge.[134] (emphasis added)

We are "primarily to act," yet when we procrastinate or practice avoidance because of fear, life will require that we are "acted upon." For example, procrastination will not delay the day a term paper is due or an exam will be given. When we take action early, wisely using our agency, we avoid cramming, will do better, and enjoy much less stress. It really is the best way to live and is enhanced when we learn how to take effective action.

Regarding acting in spite of fear, Jonathan Sandberg said, "True courage is not the absence of fear; it is the making of action in spite of fear. In order for healing to occur, we have to be courageous enough to move forward when we are afraid."[135] Taking action is better than standing still or wallowing in self-pity. However, our actions will be more effective if they are based on values and goals.

Points to Ponder: The enemies of effective action are procrastination and fear. The best way to conquer both procrastination and fear is to take action. When action is connected to our values and in alignment with our personal vision, we will be more effective and have the most joy.

Questions to Consider: What is the one thing I have desired to do, but have not started because of procrastination and/or fear? Why not start today?

Notes, thoughts, resolutions . . .

[134] *Ensign February 2006*
[135] *Sandberg, Jonathan, Brigham Young University Devotional*

"I believe in goals, but I believe that the individual should set his own. Goal setting should cause us to stretch as we make our way."
-Spencer W. Kimball

CHAPTER 15

GOALS AND OBJECTIVES

- - - - - - -

TAKE ACTION Exercise 1

If there is a secret sauce to ACT, I think it this – when we replace our top-of-mind worry with a top-of-mind goal, the worry is relegated to its proper place. Thankfully, I am a great goal setter! Why? Mostly because I have been teaching a college course on goal setting for over twenty years. I could tell you all about the reasons why goal setting is important. How SMART (specific, measurable, action oriented, realistic, time element) is a good method. I even have a whole list of obstacles and how to overcome them. But the truth is, I have mostly been lousy at goal achievement. Why? I, like most people, fall into the same trap—setting too many goals at once! As I have struggled with this whole concept, feeling very much the hypocrite, I have discovered the secret of goal setting from three very different individuals.

The first was one of our founding fathers, Benjamin Franklin. The second is a psychologist and expert on meditation and Buddhism, Rick Hanson. The third is Chris McChesney, a global consultant and execution leader with Franklin Covey. All three, in their own research and publications, have come to a similar conclusion on achievement—when it comes to goal achievement, **less is always more.**

Benjamin Franklin set out to acquire thirteen virtues, yet he chose to work on them one at a time, not taking on a new virtue until he had mastered one. Richard Hanson has a whole list of great meditation practices, yet the title of one of his books is "Just One Thing." Chris McChesney, the principal author of the "Four Disciplines of Execution" urges his readers to focus on one goal at a time. He calls this your "wildly important goal" or WIG.

In short, setting too many goals usually dooms us to achieving none. I can't tell you how many times I have fallen into this trap. Recently, I have changed my entire focus on setting goals, primarily following the model given by Chris McChesney. I have found that I am more focused, make more progress, and have much more success in achieving my goals.

As you look at your responses from the Valued Direction Exercise, you could make a very long list of things you could do or change, your own personal stops and starts. Perhaps the starts are the antidote for the stops, good habits that could replace bad habits. For example, if the stop is watching too much television, the start could be going to the temple each week. Another example: if the stop is overeating, the start could be beginning an exercise program.

Let's take a look at your values, your stops and starts, and consider what the goals or actions are that you want to work on first.

WHAT ARE YOUR MOST IMPORTANT GOALS?

In a college forum, Stephen R. Covey urged those in attendance to take some time each day to just pray, ponder, and meditate. If they let their conscience, also known as the Light of Christ, speak to them, they would know the things they should do. He specifically suggested that each ask this question: "What is the one thing I need to do to . . . be a better husband or wife or member of His church?" Participants were then asked to record the one thing they needed to work on. Let's follow this model with the values you have already listed. First, take some time to meditate and ponder on each value, all the while listening to your conscience and the whisperings of the still small voice, and then ask, "What is the one thing I need to do to? In the space below, list each value and record the one thing you need to do to take effective action.

1.   Value 1: _____
     What is the <u>one thing</u> I need to do to better live by this
     value:_____

2.   Value 2: _____
     What is the <u>one thing</u> I need to do to better live by this
     value:_____

3. Value 3: _____
    What is the <u>one thing</u> I need to do to better live by this
    value:_____

4. Value 4: _____
    What is the <u>one thing</u> I need to do to better live by this
    value:_____

5. Value 5: _____
    What is the <u>one thing</u> I need to do to better live by this
    value:_____

You should now have a list of a few action items to work on. It is very likely that because of these activities you will be more aware of things you hope to change, perhaps requiring some repentance. Because of this awareness, you will be and do better on your own accord. However, if you decide to take the next wise step of setting goals, make sure you are selective and focus on just one or two.

As you select an item to work on, take some time to write a goal achievement statement following the pattern of "from x to y by when."[136] Here is an example: "I will lose 15 pounds by March 1." Another example, "I will read the entire Book of Mormon by December 1st."

As you have identified your potential goals, take some time to ponder on which goal is the most important, perhaps even wildly important. Using the "agency" section of the worksheet, record your number one goal in the space provided. Remember to use the "from x to y by when" format.

---

[136] *McChesney, Chris, Covey, Sean, and Jim Huling. The 4 Disciplines of Execution*

	What is the one thing I must do to better live by this value?	THEREFORE
AGENCY	Write a goal statement using from X to Y by when: What are the 1-3 things I must do to achieve this goal? 1. 2. 3.	

ROADBLOCKS

Great job! You are well on your way to taking effective action on your values. Acting in alignment with your vision and values is the best antidote for worry and anxiety. Be prepared though, you will face obstacles and setbacks along the way. Let's look at the most common and explore together how to successfully proceed in spite of the barriers.

Roadblock 1 -- Impatience

Life is a journey, and not one of us will actually arrive at perfection, though that should be our ultimate eternal goal. Since we will not ever achieve perfection in any endeavor, one major roadblock is impatience. In his book "Mastery," George Leonard describes the Mastery Curve, which is illustrated in the graphic below.[137]

Love the Plateaus & the Journey

Homeostasis

---

[137] *Leonard, George. Mastery*

Whatever endeavor we undertake, we will have moments of noticeable improvement. However, in between these summits will be stretches, sometimes extended plateaus, where improvement is negligible. Let's take learning to play a musical instrument. First comes lessons, then practice, then happy moments of improvement. Often, after the growth moments, there is a bit of a dip followed by a new plateau. Overtime, if we will patiently endure the dips and times of limited improvement, growth and mastery happens. Fighting against us the whole time is the principle of homeostasis, an almost gravitational pull back to the original benchmark. Because of our impatience, many will just quit after the first or second dip or extended plateau. Leonard calls these the dabblers. Others will keep at it, but never really spend the time in practice to see improvement. These are the hackers. Finally, there are the obsessives, those who just jump from one new venture to another, never really taking the time to acquire a new talent. According to Leonard, the key to mastery is to learn to enjoy practice, to love the journey, even the plateaus between times of growth. Leonard urges those seeking mastery to understand the following keys:

1. Find good teachers
2. Practice
3. Surrender to your teachers and discipline
4. Visualize success
5. Seek your limits

Legendary basketball coach, John Wooden, summarized the value of loving the journey and practice when he said:

> In my coaching I informed every player who came under my supervision that the outcome of a game was simply the by-product of the effort we made to prepare. They understood our destination was a successful journey - namely, total, complete, and detailed preparation. Too often we neglect our journey in our eagerness or anxiety about reaching the goal.[138]

Embrace the moment, enjoy the journey, be present, and you will find peace and happiness. If you have been a chronic worrier, like me, be patient and enjoy the journey. You will not eliminate this habit in a day, a week, a

---

[138] *Wooden, John. Wooden*

month, or even a year. With practice and patience you will make steady progress and reach new levels of productivity and happiness.

Roadblock 2 -- Beware of Triggers

In spite of our best intentions, we all slip up and failure is guaranteed. Unfortunately, sometimes our missteps are actual mistakes, perhaps even sins. Repeated actions could lead to poor habits or addictions. Usually, we don't set out to make a mistake or participate in activities contrary to the Lord's spirit, but we are tempted and prone to certain triggers or enticements. Triggers can come from all sorts of places because of our awareness. Sometimes it could be as simple as a thought or perhaps activities we are involved in or even the actions of others. A useful tip is to be aware of potential triggers. The model below illustrates how triggers can cause us to go from a state of peace to guilt if we make mistakes or commit sins.

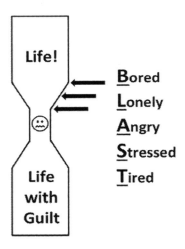

In this model, we are enjoying life with the Spirit and no real concerns. However, there is a trigger like a worried thought, something we have viewed on media, or perhaps the actions of others. If attended to, more triggers will come or perhaps the first is amplified. If this continues, it is very likely that we will succumb to the sin associated with the trigger. This is represented by the narrow gap in the model. Shortly after falling, the temptations dissipate and life opens up again but now with a heavy dose guilt. The acronym BLAST (bored, lonely, angry, stressed, or tired) is a good reminder that at times we may be more susceptible to triggers. When we are bored, lonely, angry, stressed, or tired we will be more vulnerable. The key is to have enough self-awareness to know when you are dealing with one or more of the BLAST elements and to have an action plan, almost like a to-do list. These could be things like reading from the scriptures, calling a friend, sending a message, doing ten push-ups, etc. It would even be a good idea to craft your list and post it in places as a reminder. Many of the activities discussed in this book like meditation, journaling, exercise, and service would be good to-do items as you notice and deal with your personal triggers. Make sure that as you create your to-do list, your action items are connected to your values.

Roadblock 3 -- Peer Pressure

We know peer pressure is very real for young people, but it can be an obstacle for all ages. Wanting to please our peers, to fit in, or to be esteemed by them is rooted in pride, what President Ezra Taft Benson called the "universal sin." As natural men and women, we can all easily fall prey to pride and its cousin, envy. In my class, I often conduct what I call the buttermilk experiment. It is true that my grandparents drank buttermilk, perhaps with a little salt or pepper. However, the younger generations just assume it is good in biscuits and pancakes. In fact, I have yet to meet a college age student who has actually drank straight buttermilk. In a classroom setting, I would ask the students who had tried buttermilk. No one would raise their hand. I then would ask, "Who is 100% certain they would not like to drink buttermilk?" Again, this would result in an almost universal "no" response. I would then select one student to leave the room and wait in the hall. I then told the rest of the class they would all be buttermilk advocates, with one leader. Their goal was to see how quickly they could get the person waiting in the hall to drink some buttermilk. To make matters worse, I had doctored the buttermilk with a bit of green food coloring to make it look even more unappealing. The room was set up with one small table, two chairs, the container of buttermilk, two small clear glasses, and some paper towels. I would then invite the person back into the room and have him or her sit across the table from the lead advocate. The leader and the class would then start inviting the person to drink, often mildly at first then quickly raising the stakes. The class would use all sorts of methods including heckling, bribery, teasing, and so on. Without exception,

143

and usually with the lead advocate agreeing to also drink, the student ends up partaking of green buttermilk. Gagging, spitting, and looking for a glass of water then follows.

The point of this object lesson is that peer pressure amounts to a desire to measure up, to be accepted, and can be one of the main reasons we are not always true to our values.

Roadblock 4 -- Delaying Gratification

Most of us are not very good at waiting. Have you ever watched a kid eat a Blow Pop sucker, one with candy on the outside and bubble gum in the middle? Some children will patiently enjoy the candy, taking time to enjoy every lick. Then, when they get to the gum, they have a second treat. Others just can't wait for the gum. The candy is an obstacle, and very soon they are crunching away, risking broken teeth in the process. Each day most of us have necessary, even worthwhile tasks that are simply not as much fun as others. So often we put them off until they can no longer be ignored or our level of guilt becomes so high we reluctantly act. Are any of your valued actions getting hijacked or postponed because you are too busy in the thick of thin things? The process of delaying gratification is to schedule the necessary, even vital activities that may be less enjoyable first. A perfect example is the "A" student who gets all of his or her homework done before their fun activities. They get more done, do quality work, and have guilt-free fun because they know they are not neglecting important schoolwork.

How important is overcoming worry and anxiety to you? I am confident the practices in this book can be very effective and result in real healing. Yet, they are of no value unless you take action and patiently repeat the practices until new habits of thinking and feeling are established. Don't wait and let procrastination keep this from happening. If you do nothing, you will be subject to the powerful forces of entropy.

BEWARE OF ENTROPY

The key to success is based on your capacity to stick with it until new and better habits are formed. When we live true to our values, supported by good habits, we will enjoy more productivity, happiness, and peace. As mentioned earlier, the real healing power of ACT is this: if we busy ourselves acting on our values and goals, our worries and fears just become background noise. In fact, they may never disappear totally, but they don't hold our attention or hijack our lives. However, we need to be aware of the "Law of Entropy," which states: "Life [or our values] unattended to or neglected will naturally move toward a disorganized, undifferentiated state."[139] This is true when it comes to your bedroom, desk, relationships, and even your testimony. If we want to live by our values and take effective action, we must pay attention to those things that matter most. The best way to fight entropy is to set goals, act on objectives, and return-and-report.

The next step is to determine a small list of actionable objectives that will help you achieve a goal. Chris McChesney calls it "acting on the lead measures," the activities that will both influence the outcome and predict success.[140] Just like goals, you can make the mistake of making a list of objectives that are too long. Focus on the few objectives that will lead to success. Here is an example for the weight loss goal listed previously:

Goal: I will lose 15 pounds by March 1

    Objective 1: Get a phone app to count calories and exercise activity.

    Objective 2: Get a gym membership

    Objective 3: Make a schedule and stick to it

    Objective 4: Find a workout buddy

Now that you have identified and recorded a goal to work on, it is time to make a list of the objectives, or the steps, to help you achieve your goal. Use the section on the following worksheet to record your short list of "to do" items.

---

[139] *Christensen, David. Inner Victory*
[140] *McChesney, Chris, Covey, Sean, and Jim Huling. The 4 Disciplines of Execution*

	What is the one thing I must do to better live by this value?	THEREFORE
AGENCY	Write a goal statement using from X to Y by when:	
	What are the 1-3 things I must do to achieve this goal?	
	1.	
	2.	
	3.	

Points to Ponder: We are more effective and will achieve more if we set goals. Goals are more likely to be reached when we focus on just one or two and understand the specific steps or objectives for each goal. A clear understanding of the common roadblocks will help us avoid pitfalls and have more success.

Questions to Consider: Am I a goal setter? If I could pick just one goal to work on, what would it be? What are the steps I need to take to reach that goal?

Notes, thoughts, resolutions . . .

Notes continued . . .

"The unexamined life is not worth living."
—Socrates

CHAPTER 16

ACCOUNT

- - - - - - -

TAKE ACTION Exercise 2

The final step is to create some accountability measures. This could include creating a scorecard and establishing a "report to" person. Journaling can be a very good accountability tool. Spouses, siblings or church leaders can also help with your goal stewardship. Please don't forget to record your efforts in the provided Mindfulness Activituy Log (also available at https://lessonsfromlibertyjail.com). There are also some very good apps for your smartphone or tablet that will help you track daily activity and progress. Some work very well with specific goals like weight loss, nutrition, and exercise.

President Thomas S. Monson expounds on goal setting and accountability:

> When we deal in generalities, we shall never succeed. When we deal in specifics, we shall rarely have a failure. When performance is measured, performance improves. When performance is measured and reported, the rate of performance accelerates.[141]

Often, reporting mechanisms are established in the natural framework of organizations or groups. The church is a wonderful example with weekly, monthly, and annual reports. Missionaries have multiple levels of accountability including companions, district leaders, zone leaders, and finally the mission president.

On more personal matters, it could be as simple as selecting a "workout buddy," someone with similar goals and interests. The key is

---

[141] *Ensign November 1984*

creating a routine and sticking to it until it becomes habit.

An effective tool for reporting and habit formation is the checklist. In his New York Times bestseller "The Checklist Manifesto," Dr. Atul Gawande demonstrates with real concrete examples the power of using this simple method. For example, air travel was made possible because of a simple discovery, the pre-flight checklist. Prior to this breakthrough, tragic accidents were common, dashing any hopes of commercial air travel. Likewise, healthcare practices have greatly benefitted as doctors, nurses, and others developed checklists that ensure the quality and safety of surgeries and other procedures.[142]

Can you and I benefit from having a checklist, especially as we deal with personal and spiritual matters? Elder Joe J. Christensen, in his book "To Grow in Spirit," offers a simple ten-point checklist that will help increase spirituality. Over the years I have referred to this list as a self-assessment, which usually resulted in some degree of guilt and at times motivation to do better. As an example of the value of a personal checklist, here is Elder Joe J. Christensen's "ten point plan for becoming more spiritual:"[143]

1. Do I read the scriptures daily? (2 Nephi 32:3)
2. Do I really pray and not just say prayers? (Alma 34:17-27; Matthew 6:7)
3. Is my fasting meaningful, or do I do more than just get hungry? (D&C 59:13-23)
4. Do I go to bed early and get up early? (D&C 88:124)
5. Am I essentially a happy person? (D&C 31:3)
6. Do I work hard? (D&C 4:2; D&C 31:5)
7. Am I more concerned about how than where I serve? (John 13:12-17)
8. Do I love everyone - even enemies - and keep my romantic feelings in their proper perspective? (John 13:34-35)
9. Do I strive for oneness with others as well as within myself, between my ideal and actual self? (3 Nephi 27:27; D&C 38:27)
10. Do I share my testimony with others? (D&C 33:7-10; D&C 60:2)

The checklist model used here by Elder Christensen is actually a very

---

[142] Gawande, Atul. The Checklist Manifesto
[143] Christensen, Joe J. To Grow in Spirit

common practice amongst leaders of the Church. Often, especially in General Conference, inspired speakers will offer short to-do lists, like this example from President Thomas S. Monson:

> May I suggest three imperatives for our consideration. They are within our reach. A kind Heavenly Father will help us in our quest. First, learn what we should learn. Second, do what we should do. And third, be what we should be.[144]

And this example from President Gordon B. Hinckley:

> Now I offer you a very simple recipe which, if observed, will assure your happiness. It is a simple four-point program. It is as follows: (1) pray, (2) study, (3) pay your tithing, and (4) attend your meetings.[145]

As you consider your vision, values, goals, and objectives, would it be useful to create your own personal checklist? The habit of reviewing our purpose and actions daily will help fight the constant pull of entropy and ensure that we are living true to our vision and purpose.

Points to Ponder: We will achieve more if we have accountability and can report progress. Scorecards and checklists can be valuable if they are used on a regular basis and include an accountability steward like a mentor.

Questions to Consider: Do I have mentor? How could I benefit from a personal scorecard or checklist? Who would be a good person to report to regarding my progress?

Notes, thoughts, resolutions . . .

---

[144] *Ensign November 2008*
[145] *Ensign May 2007*

"The gospel of Jesus Christ is simply beautiful and beautifully simple."
—Matthew Cowley

CHAPTER 17

THE FINAL THEREFORE (D&C 123:17)

The ultimate promise from Liberty Jail is that we can have peace knowing that the Lord will consecrate all of our trials for our good. The last scripture in these revelations provides the final **therefore** in the Liberty Jail revelations,[146] and it just might contain the secret to solving almost all of our problems—the ultimate self-help in just thirty-eight words. I have referred to this as my safety net scripture. If we are living the gospel, including receiving all of the saving ordinances, we cannot fail. Heavenly Father will not allow it and will not short us on any of the blessings we were foreordained to receive, nor will He limit us from becoming all that we are to become. If we are faithful, there is no need to worry. While personal trials may naturally cause anxious feelings, these will be "but a small moment and "shall be for [our] good."[147]

Let's take an in-depth look at Doctrine and Covenants 123:17 and consider how the Lord will help us overcome worry and anxiety, assisted by the simple tools of ACT. The Lord states, "Therefore dearly beloved, let us cheerfully do all things that lie in our power and then may we stand still, with the utmost assurance. To see the hand of God and for His arm to be revealed."

Therefore, dearly beloved -- We are loved of our Heavenly Father. We are all His children, and this is the most important "know."

Let Us -- We are not in this alone. "Us" includes our family, friends, church members, Heavenly Father, His Son, and the Holy Ghost. As we follow the

---

[146] *Doctrine and Covenants 123:17*
[147] *Doctrine and Covenants 121:7*

principles and practices of **if, know, therefore** and ACT, we will be more effective if we have partners.

<u>Cheerfully</u> -- President Dieter F. Uchtdorf taught that we should be grateful in any circumstance. He said:

> It is easy to be grateful for things when life seems to be going our way. But what then of those times when what we wish for seems to be far out of reach?
>
> Could I suggest that we see gratitude as a disposition, a way of life that stands independent of our current situation? In other words, I'm suggesting that instead of being thankful for things, we focus on being thankful in our circumstances—whatever they may be.[148]

Cheerfulness as a disposition is a habit worth cultivating and is made easier when we practice the mindfulness skills of acceptance and embracing the moment, living in the "holy present."

<u>Do all Things that Lie in our Power</u> -- We should be anxiously engaged, acting on those things we value, in alignment with our vision. Our actions will be enhanced as we seek to follow the two great commandments, putting God first and then serving His children (the JOY principle).

<u>Then May We Stand Still</u> -- When we take time to ponder and meditate, creating a gap or space between "life happening and our responses to life happening," we increase our capacity to be led by the Light of Christ and the Holy Ghost. This helps us "mind the gap" between stimulus and response, allowing us to do more because of the enabling power of the Atonement, even being healed by His grace.

<u>With the Utmost Assurance</u> -- Faith is the first principle of the gospel and "utmost assurance" implies we will "Trust in the Lord with all [our] heart[s]; and lean not unto [our] own understanding."[149] All worry is based on "unlikely maybe's" and rooted in fear. Faith is the opposite of fear, and trust in the Lord gives us a greater capacity to act on our values, relegating worry to its proper place.

---

[148] *Ensign May 2014*
[149] *Proverbs 3:5*

<u>To See the Salvation of God and, for His Arm to Be Revealed</u> -- As we exercise faith, practice patience, and do our part, we will sense His presence and know His will.

In our lives, especially as we look back, we will remember times when we saw the "salvation of the Lord" and "His arm . . . revealed." In my life I have had several, but one in particular stands out as proof positive God would not let me mess up and miss out on any of my foreordained blessings. Anyone who visits our home, my office, or even our family blog will notice a little diversity in our family. Our fourth son is adopted and is African American. While that alone is not really a big deal, especially in the 21st Century, how this unfolded for us as a family, and for me personally, is a testimony of divine assistance. We had our "ifs and whens," were blessed to "know," and almost naively practiced some good "therefores."

When my wife and I started on our marriage journey, we talked fondly about our ideal family. Hopefully, just like her family with six children, three boys and three girls, all spaced out just right. Sadly, like many couples just making a plan and hoping for a child did not automatically guarantee success. After a few frustrating years, with lots of worry, research and trips to the doctor, we learned we were sub-fertile, which we guessed was better than infertile. We were assured that with some medical intervention, we could conceive. Being very poor college students, we decided to just wait one more year until I graduated from college and secured employment. We even dropped our maternity insurance, officially stopped trying and promptly got pregnant. Our first happy experience with "acceptance" and perhaps "paradoxical intent."

Over the next several years, we welcomed two more children into our home, and suffered the loss of one stillborn son. However, the spaces between each child were much longer than we had hoped, with return trips to seek medical assistance. And, just like with child number one, conception happened after we quit trying, thanks in large part to a wise friend and LDS counselor who told us to just take a month off with the direct order of "hugs and kisses only." The next pregnancy happened after a doctor told us he had a sure fire solution, but we decided to postpone the procedure until after our planned summer trip to Disneyland. Again, a preview of ACT, we quit trying (attachment) and accepted our current fate.

After some time we settled into a very happy life with our family in Idaho. While we still hoped for more children, we tried to pretend we were not trying. I began to justify the size of our family by researching many of those, including two modern day prophets, who had small families. We were going to be okay. That was until our daughter started praying for a sister. Every family prayer she offered included this plea. After nearly a decade of these prayers and realizing her parents were not likely to get pregnant, she began to pray we would adopt.

Adoption! Of course my wife was all for this, but I was definitely not. You see, I adored my kids, but mostly just tolerated others. I doubted I could care for a kid that was not biologically ours. Plus, I am a huge cheapskate and adoption was very, very expensive. I would list a dozen reasons why we were okay and even more why adoption was a foolish choice. Over the next few years, I patiently endured the prayers and adoption talk saying to myself, "this too shall pass." Through this process, both my awareness and blind spots were working full force. I noticed those who had adopted children and generally focused on the negatives.

I finally relented to at least allow a home study to be done and even helped my wife research different options. In the middle of all of this, almost miraculously and again paradoxically, we became pregnant for the fifth time. However, from the beginning this pregnancy was different with much less morning sickness, which we tried to brush off as a blessing from heaven. Within just a few weeks my wife miscarried and we were squarely back to the adoption question. However, this time I was more on board and even created a profile on a website called "Hope to Adopt."

Within just a few days, we had our first promising contact from a young LDS lady in New Mexico. She was going to have a baby girl and we were her first choice – a sister was coming! We corresponded, made plans, and even canceled my wife's trip with me to Europe. As the time drew closer, we started to talk about getting attorneys involved and determining the steps we would need to finalize a private adoption. Suddenly, however, the communication from our prospective birth mother just stopped. I finally sent a pretty direct email to our supposed birth mother and this time did get a response with the shocking news she never was pregnant, just lonely and needed some attention. She apologized and told us she was seeking professional help. To say we were disappointed was an understatement -- and any inclination I had to adopt was officially shot. Well, my wife was still "hoping to adopt" and my daughter's prayers kept on in earnest.

Because I enrolled on the "Hope to Adopt" web service, we were subscribed to some adoption email lists. One morning I was at my desk working when I received an email from an adoption agency. The message stated that they had just learned of a baby that was going to be born within the month and they needed to find a family right away. The need was so great they were even offering a discounted price. This email piqued my interest, but I quickly discounted it because this soon-to-be-born baby was an African American boy and we were hoping for a mixed race or Caucasian girl. For several moments my mouse and cursor icon hovered over the delete button. I knew by sharing this message with my family, especially my wife and daughter, there could be hours of discussion, even pleadings. I knew I would be ganged up on as the supposed voice of reason. If I hit delete, I would be spared, yet I printed the email and shared the message.

True to my prediction, the discussions at home began in earnest and I was obviously the odd-man-out. I was still skeptical of adoption, especially since the gender did not match our plans and an agency adoption would be very expensive. After a few days, and on a Sunday evening, I exercised some patriarchal dad's-in-charge authority and called a family council. I asked everyone's opinion, which included my wife, daughter, and youngest son. The only one missing was our eldest son who was serving a full-time mission. All were positively in favor so I decided to forcefully state my opinion in opposition. I argued this type of adoption was risky, expensive, and not in line with our initial plans. I told them that I wanted to drop the issue and we were not going to volunteer as candidates for this little boy. Apparently my argument was strong enough and there was reluctant, even resigned acceptance. I went to bed feeling like I had finally put this issue to rest.

I arose the next morning and followed my usual routine, including the short three-block walk to work. Along the way, I was somewhat perplexed because I felt particularly anxious, almost like I was sick to my stomach. I arrived at work and settled in at my desk, still pondering why I felt so poorly. I rationalized that perhaps I was a bit strong in my rhetoric during the family council from the night before and knowing I had dashed the hopes of people I loved. I felt like I needed at least one companion on my side, so I quickly composed an email to our missionary son. My email said something like, "Dear Elder, what do you think of the possibility of having an African American baby brother?" You see, before my son's mission, he and I shared similar feelings that our little family with three living children, and one in heaven, was really okay. I impatiently waited through the morning because Monday was our email day. Our son and his message would surely support my position and "ease my pain." Well, the message came and to my surprise he stated he would welcome a new baby brother and felt "really good" about the idea. I was now very much alone and my angst was even stronger. I quickly called my wife and asked her how she was doing. She expressed that she was feeling poorly and when I asked her to describe her symptoms, they were very much like my own. At that moment I learned the Lord can and will answer your prayers with very strong "negative" impressions and emotions. I literally felt like I had been kicked in the stomach and I knew that my decision to opt out of this opportunity was incorrect. My wife and I concluded the Lord's message to us was crystal clear and we should pursue this chance for a new baby. Almost instantly, our anxious feelings disappeared and we both felt peace.

We now started the adoption proceedings with the agency in earnest. After completing all of the necessary paperwork, we soon learned that the birth mother had narrowed her list of potential families to three, and we were on that list! Our chances looked pretty good! Sadly, we soon learned the birth mother had selected another family. We were shocked and wondered why would the Lord gave us such strong spiritual promptings only to be denied? We surmised that perhaps the Lord was telling us, and particularly me, that pursuing adoption really would be okay. Still, this was a bitter pill to swallow since we now had two failures.

One night, I was shopping at a local grocery store when I received a phone call from the agency. The gentleman calling informed me the family the birth mother had chosen had two offers and they had decided to select the other baby. We were now first on the list and this new baby boy could be ours. I immediately said yes, even without asking my wife, and quickly called her to tell her the happy news. The challenge, this baby boy was going to be born the next day and we needed to get my wife to Atlanta right away. I rushed home and immediately got on the computer to secure a flight from Salt Lake City, Utah to Atlanta, Georgia, and within just hours we were on the road to Utah.

While I was very much used to traveling, including reservations, airports, rental cars, and hotels, this was new for my wife. She was justifiably very nervous, put bravely forged ahead. Thanks to several tender mercies, she arrived safely.

What followed was a whirlwind of events as my wife met birth parents, the birth grandmother, and a brand new baby boy. Upon meeting my wife, the grandmother excitedly exclaimed that she was "just as she imagined." My wife then met the birth mother and baby, and she was also excited to meet my wife. Sadly, the birth father wanted no part of it and refused to meet this intruder from Idaho. My wife was very patient and encouraged the mother and grandmother to take some time to reflect, ponder, and pray. She even took the opportunity to teach the basics of the Plan of Salvation. As it was the middle of the day, she offered to buy everyone lunch and she hurried off. Once she returned, the birth father was now willing to meet and surprisingly he and my wife made an immediate connection. Within a short time, and we believe because of real promptings from the Spirit, they all decided to proceed with the adoption stating, "You need to hold him because he is your baby." Soon, the attorney arrived to complete the necessary paperwork and he escorted my wife and the baby to her rental car. Along the way, he shared that in all of his work with adoptions he had never felt the feelings he experienced in that hospital room. He said, "I'm not sure why I feel this way, but that is your baby." Well, we know why and are confident that everyone involved, including a non-LDS attorney, were feeling the promptings of the Holy Spirit.

Within a few days, my wife and our new son made it out west and he was united with two of his older siblings. Now it was time for my paradigm shifts! This was our fifth child, my fourth son, and I got to see and hold him for the first time in the middle of a flood of people in the Salt Lake City Airport. It was so different and I was concerned those wonderfully intimate feelings were not immediate. Thankfully, I was amazed at how soon we bonded and that my feelings of affection were no different than with my other children.

Over the next few months we enjoyed three very sacred experiences. The first was in our local courthouse as our family became official. The second was the baby blessing. And the final grand day happened in the temple as our son was sealed to us as his parents.

After a couple of years, my wife and I started discussing the need for our son to have a sibling and of course adoption would be the likely avenue. This time, I would be all in! We were even willing to take on more debt. However, one day at the kitchen sink my wife heard the words in her mind, "you are expecting." What?! It had been over a decade since our last successful pregnancy. I was convinced our fertile days were long gone. Plus, I was approaching 47 and my wife 44 -- no way could we be expecting! A few months later, we welcomed a new daughter into our home. My oldest daughter finally had a baby sister. After 24 years of marriage and a span of 22 years from our oldest son, to our youngest daughter, we ended up with our 6 children. Not a perfect split of three of each, but we will take our four and two and happily look forward to the day when we will have a reunion with the son we lost.

At no time during this whole process were we perfect and always cheerful. Did we always "stand still" with "utmost assurance?" No. Yet, through our entire married life we have strived to be obedient and with hope accepted what "came our way." We, especially our young children, never stopped praying and asking for the Lord's help. Somewhere, in the grand design for our family, it was in the plan all along for us to find and adopt our son. For sure, we could have messed it up because of a lack of faith or disobedience, but thankfully we lived our lives well enough to "see the salvation of God and for His arm to be revealed."

Therefore, for you and for me, if we will cheerfully "hold on", "fear not," and do "all things in our power," there is really no need to worry, fuss, or live in fear. We will receive every blessing God has in store for us. As we gain the skill of "standing still," accepting and embracing all life brings, we will witness His hand in our lives.

Points to Ponder: Heavenly Father has a plan for each of us. We all have foreordained blessings and opportunities. These are dependent on our faithfulness and are guaranteed as long as we cheerfully do all we can, trust in Him, and patiently wait for His will to be revealed.

Questions to Consider: As I reflect on my life, what are the times when His hand has guided me? How can I more cheerfully do all I can, trust in Him, and be still (even through hard times) to see His salvation and hand revealed?

Notes, thoughts, resolutions . . .

List of Terms

Acceptance- Acceptance comes from stopping and recognizing unpleasant thought and feelings, and learning how to accept those thoughts.

Acceptance and Commitment Therapy (ACT)- This is a new mental health theory developed by Steven C. Hayes that utilizes three steps to overcoming anxiety and depression, designed to create psychological flexibility. These steps are accepting your thoughts, choosing your values, and taking action.

BLAST- This acronym stands for bored, lonely, angry, stressed, and tired. BLAST is a good reminder of moments when we are more likely to fall susceptible to triggers that make one more susceptible to bad habits.

Cognitive Behavior Therapy- Cognitive Behavior Therapy is a form of psychotherapy. It was originally designed to treat depression, but is now used for a number of mental disorders. It works to solve current problems and change unhelpful thinking and behavior.

CRAFT- This acronym stands for "cancel, replace, affirm, focus, train." By cancelling all negative thoughts and replacing them with positive thoughts; then by affirming those positive thoughts and visualize success, you can train yourself to change your mindset. This is a classical approach to cognitive behavior therapy.

FEAR- This acronym stands for fusion with memories, thoughts and images, evaluating your experience, avoiding your experiences, and reasons for your behavior.

HEAL- This acronym stands for having a positive experience, enhancing that experience, absorbing it, and linking the positive with the negative.

JOY- The path to having joy in our lives can be found by putting Jesus first, others second, and yourself last.

Meditation- The act or process of spending time in quiet thought. This can be done many ways but, as pointed out in the book, one successful way to meditate is by focusing your thoughts on your breathing, increasing the capacity to be still and not attached to unwanted thoughts and feelings.

Mindfulness- A mental state achieved by focusing one's awareness on the present moment, while calmly acknowledging and accepting one's feelings, thoughts, and bodily sensations, used as a therapeutic technique.

Paradigms- An intellectual perception or view, accepted by an individual or a society as a clear example, model, or pattern of how things work in the world.

Perception- The ability to see, hear, or become aware of something through the senses.

Scotomas- A partial loss of vision or a blind spot in an otherwise normal visual field.

SMART- This acronym stands for specific, measurable, action oriented, realistic, time element.

STA^{2}R- A simple practice that incorporates the core elements of ACT and includes the steps of stop, take a deep breath, accept things as they are, ask what you really want, and react in a positive way.

Stimulus Response- Stimulus Response is a concept in psychology that refers to the belief that behavior manifests as a result of the interplay between stimulus and response.

The Golden Mean- The Golden Mean is the desirable middle between two extremes, one of excess and the other of deficiency. For example, in the Aristotelian view, courage is a virtue, but if taken to excess would manifest as recklessness, and, in deficiency, cowardice.

WAFs- This is an acronym for worry, anxiety and fear. It was developed by Forsyth and Eifert.

Works Cited (listed in alphabetical order by author)

- Achor, Shawn. The Happiness Advantage: The Seven Principles of Positive Psychology That Fuel Success and Performance at Work: Crown Business, 2010.
- Chodron, Pema. Taking the Leap: Freeing Ourselves from Old Habits and Fears: Shambhala, 2010.
- Christensen, Clayton. How will You Measure Your Life?: Harper Business, 2012.
- Christensen, David. Inner Victory: Capacity Books, 1995.
- Christensen, Joe J. To Grow in Spirit: Deseret Book, 1989.
- Covey, Stephen. The 7 Habits of Highly Effective People: Simon Schuster Ltd Uk, 1990.
- The Church of Jesus Christ of Latter-day Saints Handbook 2: Administering the Church.
- Forsyth, John P. and Eifert, Georg H. The Mindfulness and Acceptance Workbook for Anxiety: A Guide to Breaking Free from Anxiety, Phobias, and Worry Using Acceptance and Commitment Therapy: New Harbinger Publications, 2008.
- Frankl, Victor. Man's Search for Meaning: Washington Square Press, 1984.
- Gawande, Atul. The Checklist Manifesto: How to Get Things Right: Metropolitan Books, 2009.
- Hanson, Rick. Just One Thing: Developing a Buddha Brain One Simple Practice at a Time: New Harbinger Publications, 2011.
- Hanson, Rick. Hardwiring Happiness: The New Brain Science of Contentment, Calm, and Confidence: Harmony, 2013.
- Harris, Russ. The Happiness Trap: How to Stop Struggling and Start Living: A Guide to ACT, Trumpeter, 2008.
- Hayes, Steven. Get Out of Your Mind and Into Your Life: The New Acceptance and Commitment Therapy (A New Harbinger Self-Help Workbook) First Edition: Harbinger Publications, 2005.
- Hoffman, Jan. Anxious Students Strain College Mental Health Centers: New York Times, May 27, 2015.
- Hunt, Jason. Self Control; As Easy as Selflessness?: http://www.byui.edu/alumni/webcasts, 2015.
- Jones, Dewitt. http://www.celebratewhatsright.com.
- Kabat-Zinn, Jon. Full Catastrophe Living: Using the Wisdom of Your Body & Mind to Face Stress, Pain & Illness: Delta, 2009.

- Kabat-Zinn, Jon. Mindfulness for Beginners: Reclaiming the Present Moment--and Your Life: Sounds True, 2011.
- Kimball, Spencer W. The Miracle of Forgiveness: Bookcraft, 1969.
- Kimball, Spencer W. The Teachings of Spencer W. Kimball, Twelfth President of the Church of Jesus Christ of Latter-day Saints: Bookcraft, 1995.
- Klemp, Harold. The Book of ECK Parables, Volume. 2: Illuminated Way Publishing, 1988.
- Leonard, George. Mastery: The Keys to Success and Long-Term Fulfillment: Plume, 1992.
- Maltz, Maxwell: Psycho-cybernetics, A New Way to Get More Living Out of Life: Pocket Books, 1989.
- Mandino, Og. The Greatest Salesman in the World: Bantam, 1983.
- Marx, Jeffrey. Season of Life: A Football Star, a Boy, a Journey to Manhood: Simon & Schuster, 2004.
- McChesney, Chris, Covey, Sean, and Jim Huling. The 4 Disciplines of Execution: Achieving Your Wildly Important Goals: Free Press, 2012.
- Peck, M. Scott. The Road Less Traveled, Timeless Edition: A New Psychology of Love, Traditional Values and Spiritual Growth: Walker, 1978
- Purse, Gary. Abiding in the Still Lands: http://www.byui.edu/alumni/webcasts, 2015.
- Rasband, Ester. Confronting the Myth of Self-Esteem: Twelve Keys to Finding Peace: Deseret Book, 1998.
- Rinpoche, Yongey Mingyur and Swanson, Eric. The Joy of Living: Harmony, 2008.
- Rossman, Martin. The Worry Solution: Using Breakthrough Brain Science to Turn Stress and Anxiety into Confidence and Happiness: Harmony, 2010.
- Sandberg, Jonathan. https://speeches.byu.edu/talks/jonathan-g-sandberg_healing-courage-action-grace/: 2014.
- Sayers, Gale. I Am Third: The Inspiration for Brian's Song: Penguin Books, 2001.
- Sommer, Bobbe. Psycho-cybernetics 2000: Prentice Hall, 2000.
- Williams, Nathan. If, Know, Therefore: http://www.byui.edu/alumni/webcasts, 2015.

- Wooden, John. Wooden: A Lifetime of Observations and Reflections On and Off the Court: Contemporary Books, 1997.
- Wrigley, Carrie M., Christ Centered Healing From Depression and Low Self Worth: www.byutv.org/.../byu-education-week-carrie-m-wrigley-2005.

Worksheets

IF	PEACE		
VISION	My Personal Mission Statement:		KNOW
	The values from my mission statement are:		
	One of my important values is:		**J O Y**
	Importance:		
	0 — Not important	3 — Moderately Important	5 — Very Important
	Satisfaction:		
	0 — Not Satisfied	3 — Moderately Satisfied	5 — Very Satisfied
	Is there a discrepancy? If so, why?		
	Are there things I should stop or start doing?		
AGENCY	What is the one thing I must do to better live by this value?		THEREFORE
	Write a goal statement using from X to Y by when:		
	What are the 1-3 things I must do to achieve this goal?		
	1.		
	2.		
	3.		
	BECOME		

IF	PEACE	
	My Personal Mission Statement:	KNOW

The values from my mission statement are:

VISION

One of my important values is:

J O Y

Importance: _____

0   3   5

Not important   Moderately Important   Very Important

Satisfaction: _____

0   3   5

Not Satisfied   Moderately Satisfied   Very Satisfied

Is there a discrepancy? If so, why?

Are there things I should stop or start doing?

What is the one thing I must do to better live by this value?	THEREFORE

AGENCY

Write a goal statement using from X to Y by when:

What are the 1-3 things I must do to achieve this goal?

1.

2.

3.

BECOME

IF	PEACE	
VISION	My Personal Mission Statement:	**KNOW**
	The values from my mission statement are:	
	One of my important values is:	**J O Y**

Importance: _____
             0   3   5
      Not important   Moderately Important   Very Important

Satisfaction: _____
             0   3   5
      Not Satisfied   Moderately Satisfied   Very Satisfied

Is there a discrepancy? If so, why?

Are there things I should stop or start doing?

AGENCY	What is the one thing I must do to better live by this value?	**THEREFORE**
	Write a goal statement using from X to Y by when:	
	What are the 1-3 things I must do to achieve this goal?	
	1.	
	2.	
	3.	

BECOME

IF	PEACE	
	My Personal Mission Statement:	KNOW

The values from my mission statement are:

One of my important values is: **J O Y**

Importance: _____
0   3   5
Not important   Moderately Important   Very Important

Satisfaction: _____
0   3   5
Not Satisfied   Moderately Satisfied   Very Satisfied

Is there a discrepancy? If so, why?

Are there things I should stop or start doing?

VISION (vertical label)

What is the one thing I must do to better live by this value?   **THEREFORE**

Write a goal statement using from X to Y by when:

What are the 1-3 things I must do to achieve this goal?

1.

2.

3.

AGENCY (vertical label)

BECOME

Mindfulness Activity Log

Month:			

Activity: STA²R , Mindful Breathing, Observing (mind watching), Expansion, Urge Surfing, Mindful Eating, Mindful Walking, Observing Others, Notice 5 Things, HEAL

Bridle Meditations: Be Still, Remember, Serve, or Let Go.

Day	Activity	Time Spent	Thoughts

Liberty Jail, a Synopsis:

Photo credit: LDS Media Library, taken 1896.

History

The original jail was built in 1833. For season it was used as a home before being demolished. The basement room (former prison cell) was used as an ice house. The property was purchased by the Church in 1939 and the museum with the partially reconstructed jail was created in 1963.

Detainees:

Joseph Smith, Hyrum Smith, Sidney Rigdon, Lyman Wight, and Alexander McRae.

Duration:

December 1838 to April 1839, four and one-half months.

Prison Size:

Exterior – twenty-two and a half feet long, twenty-two feet wide, and twelve feet tall. Two small barred windows. The exterior wall was two-feet thick stone, the interior wall was one foot thick of solid wood. Between the stone and the wood, there was loose rubble.

Inside – fourteen by fourteen feet, with a ceiling just over six feet high in the lower basement dungeon and seven feet in the upper room.

Contributing professionals:

Dallas Johnson is a Psychologist in the BYU-Idaho Counseling Center. He previously worked in private practice and for the Veteran's Administration Hospital in Salt Lake City, Utah. He met and married Melanie Magnuson while attending the University of Utah. They have six children and live in Rexburg, Idaho.

Gary A. Purse is a professor of Religion and Philosophy at BYU-Idaho with an emphasis in World Religions--particularly teachings of the Buddha. He has a passion for teaching meditation and mindfulness and shared his practices in the webcast "Abiding in the Stillands." He and his wife Martha are the parents of 5 children and 3 grandchildren.

Nathan Williams is a professor in the Religion Department at BYU-Idaho. He shared the lecture "If, Know, Therefore" as part of the BYU-Idaho Alumni Webcast series. He served a mission to Denver, Colorado and is married to Laurie Bevans from Cardston, Alberta, Canada. They have 5 children.

Made in the USA
San Bernardino, CA
27 June 2016